McNeil Island Cemeteries:

Settlers and Prisoners

Introduction

This book is about the forgotten cemeteries on McNeil Island. In all, McNeil Island has had three cemeteries and one gravesite on it. The first cemetery was started when the island had a territory prison in about 1879. It was started to bury the prisoners that died while in prison. The settlers who lived on the island at this time were buried on their farms or in a cemetery on the mainland. The first periment US Penitentiary building was built next to the cemetery. Because of needed growth for the penitentiary it was decided to move the prisoner bodies to a new cemetery. So in 1904 a new prisoner cemetery was made and the bodies were moved to their new resting place. The settlers also decided that they needed a cemetery on the island in 1905. By 1938 the federal government had purchased most of the island and the settlers were already gone or were told they had to leave. They wanted to be able to visit their loved ones buried at the cemetery so it was decided to move the bodies to cemeteries of the families choosing, So from 1937 to 1938 all the settlers buried in the settlers cemetery were moved to other cemeteries. At this time there is the prisoners cemetery and the grave of one little boy who was buried on his family farm under four trees that had grown together. Because they were worried that the roots of the trees were around the grave, the government allowed the boy's body to stay and put a clause in their rules about visitors to the island that the family would always be able to visit little Edwin's grave. Edwin William Holm was born in August 1895 and died in May 1896. The information about the settlers and prisoners who were or are buried on McNeil Island came mostly from prison receiving books, death certificates, McNeil Island disinterment permits, World War I and II draft cards and census records. For Prison records on
Ancestry.com https://www.ancestry.com/search/collections/1253/ or on FamilySearch.org
https://www.familysearch.org/search/catalog/453527?availability=Family%20History%20Library
for death certificates
https://www.familysearch.org/search/catalog/179363?availability=Family%20History%20Library
For obituaries https://www.newspapers.com/ and https://chroniclingamerica.loc.gov/
For WWI draft records https://www.familysearch.org/search/collection/1968530
For WWII draft records https://www.familysearch.org/search/collection/1861144
For census records go to https://www.ancestry.com/search/categories/35/ then type in the year you want or
https://www.familysearch.org/search/catalog/results?count=20&placeId=337&query=%2Bplace%3A%22United%20States%22 then scroll the year you want. For the state disinterment permits
https://www.digitalarchives.wa.gov/Search# then for record series type Misc Family History, next county Pierce and the title is McNeil Island Disinterment Permits Issued 1938

The Washington State Archives has a list of 86 Settlers who lived and were buried on McNeil Island. 80 of these Settlers in a digital list and the other 6 I had to go to the archives to get the information. As the Federal Government bought more and more of the Island for the US Penitentiary the settlers were moving off the Island. The last few settlers were told they had to leave because of intimate domain. The Settlers Cemetery was then disinterred and the people were moved to Cemeteries that the families choose. A couple of the people I found, because of death certificates and find-a grave. They are listed in alphabetical order by last name. Most of the settlers living on the island were farmers. So, If I don't list an occupation you will know they are farmers and housewives.

1. **Anderson, Andrew**: born on 10 Jan 1860 in Sweden. He died 20 Dec 1911 in Tacoma and was buried on 22 Dec 1911 on McNeil Island. His body was moved to the Trinity Lutheran Cemetery in Parkland, Pierce, Washington. on 7 Oct 1937. Andrew was married to a lady who's name starts with an F.

2. **Anderson, Andrew**: born on 20 Jan 1860 in Sweden. He died 20 Dec 1911 in Tacoma and was buried 1911 on McNeil Island, His body was moved on 7 Oct 1937 to Anderson Cemetery in East Stanwood, Snohomish, Washington. The only record I found for Andrew is the Disinterment Permit in the State Archives.

3. **Anderson, Anna**: born in 1860 in Norway. She died 19 May 1912 in Gertrude, McNeil Island, Pierce, Washington and was buried on 22 May 1912 on McNeil Island. Gertrude was an area on McNeil Island. Anna's body was later moved to Trinity Lutheran Cemetery in Parkland, Pierce, Washington. Anderson was her married name.

4. **Anderson, Caroline**: born 8 Dec 1844 in Sweden. She died 17 Dec 1926 in Gertrude, Pierce, Washington and was buried on 20 Dec 1926 on McNeil Island. Caroline's body was moved to Trinity Lutheran Cemetery in Parkland, Pierce, Washington on 2 June 1937. Caroline was married to Nels Anderson. She immigrated in 1887. Her maiden name is Olson

5. **Anderson, Christina**: born 1 Jan 1859 in Sweden. She died 22 Mar 1925 in Tacoma, Pierce, Washington and buried on McNeil Island, Christina's body was moved 29 Mar 1938 in Trinity Lutheran Cemetery in Parkland, Pierce, Washington, Her parents are Ole Forsberg and Louisa Carlson.

6. **Anderson, Hans**: born 28 Nov 1845 in Saetre, Hurum, Buskerud, Norway. He died 21 Oct 1907 on Meridian, McNeil Island, Pierce, Washington and was buried 23 Oct 1907 on McNeil Island. Hans's body was moved 25 May 1935 in the Tacoma Cemetery in Tacoma, Pierce, Washington. His wife was Carolina.

7. **Anderson, Milton**: died on McNeil Island. Milton's body was moved on 7 Oct 1937 to Anderson Cemetery in East Stanwood, Snohomish, Washington. The only record I found for Milton is the Disinterment Permit in the State Archives.

8. **Anderson, Nels S**: born 8 Dec 1843 in Sweden. He died 7 Jan 1929 on McNeil Island and was buried 9 Jan 1929. Milton's body was moved on 2 June 1937 to Trinity Lutheran Cemetery in Parkland, Pierce, Washington. He was married to Carolina Anderson, who died 3 years earlier.

9. **Belfridge, Herbert Theos**: born 14 December 1908 in Gertrude, Pierce, Washington. He died 29 Apr 1910 at his family home on McNeil Island, Pierce, Washington. He was buried 1 May 1910 on McNeil Island, Pierce, Washington. Herbert's body was moved from 1937 to 1938 to Trinity Lutheran Cemetery in Parkland, Pierce, Washington. His parents are Alvin Karlsson Belfridge and Charlotte Nancy Seagrave.

10. **Carlson, Carl Gustav:** born 12 July 1895 in Tacoma, Pierce, Washington. He died 7 Feb 1921 in Tacoma, Pierce, Washington and was buried on McNeil Island, Pierce, Washington. Carl's body was moved on 24 May 1937 in Trinity Lutheran Cemetery, Parkland, Pierce, Washington. His parents are Albert and Amanda Carlson. He was medium height, medium built, brown eyes, and black hair. He was a farmer and supported both of his parents.

11. **Carlson, infant boy**: born 19 Mar 1910 in Tacoma, Pierce, Washington. He died 19 Mar 1910 in Tacoma, Pierce, Washington and was buried on 21 Mar 1910 on McNeil Island, Pierce, Washington. This boy's body was moved on 8 Apr 1938, to Trinity Lutheran Cemetery, in Parkland, Pierce, Washington. His parents are Gus Carlson and Emma Turine Kammen.

12. **Carlson, Mabel S**: born 24 May 1898 in Tacoma, Pierce, Washington. She died 19 July 1913 in Gertrude, Pierce, Washington and was buried 23 July 1913 on McNeil Island, Pierce, Washington. Mable's body was moved on 24 May 1937 to Trinity Lutheran Cemetery in Parkland, Pierce, Washington. Her parents are Albert and Amanda Carlson.

13. **Chapman, Joan**: born 10 Dec 1931 in Tacoma, Pierce, Washington. She died 17 Dec 1931 in Tacoma, Pierce, Washington, and was buried on McNeil Island. Joan's body was moved on 3 Aug 1937 to New Tacoma Cemetery in University Place, Pierce, Washington. Her parents are Robert Chapman and Blanche Harrison. She is listed on the Disinterment Permit as infant Chapman.

14. **Chapman, Irwin Wilbur** (known as Jack): born 25 May 1915 in McNeil Island, Pierce, Washington. He died 26 Apr 1922 in Steilacoom, Pierce, Washington and was buried on McNeil Island. Irwin's body was moved on 3 Aug 1937 to New Tacoma Cemetery in University Place, Pierce, Washington. His parents are Robert Chapman and Blanche Harriman.

15. **Edris, Alma**: born 15 May 1881 in Missouri. She died on 15 Feb 1916 in Gertrude, McNeil Island, Pierce, Washington and was buried 16 Feb 1916 on McNeil Island, Pierce, Washington. Alma's body was moved on 9 Nov 1937 to Trinity Lutheran Cemetery in Parkland, Pierce, Washington. Her parents are Daniel Shoop and Marsha Brower. She married 24 Feb 1904 to Calvin Syms Edris in Adair, Missouri.

16. **Edris Calvin Syms**: born 17 Dec 1876 in Pennsylvania. He died 16 Jan 1922 on Gertrude, McNeil Island, Pierce, Washington and was buried on 19 Jan 1922 on McNeil Island. Calvin's body was moved on 9 Nov 1937 to Trinity Lutheran Cemetery in Parkland, Pierce, Washington. He married 24 Feb 1904 to Alma Shoop in Adair, Missouri.

17. **Ellison, Irene Grace**: born 25 Dec 1898 in Wisconsin. She died on 2 Nov 1923 in Tacoma, Pierce, Washington and was buried on 5 Nov 1923 on McNeil Island. Irene's body was moved on 26 Aug 1937 to Trinity Lutheran Cemetery in Parkland, Pierce, Washington. Her parents are Albert Westron and Selma Beyer. She was married to Arthur Ellison.

18. **Fallberg, Martha**: born 15 Sep 1865 in Sweden. She died 27 Aug 1926 in Tacoma, Pierce, Washington and was buried 30 August 1926 on McNeil Island. Martha's body was moved in Apr 1938 to Trinity Lutheran Cemetery in Parkland, Pierce, Washington. Her father was John Fallberg.

19. **Finwick, John**: born 25 Mar 1873 in Norway. He died on 16 Feb 1908 in Tacoma, Pierce, Washington and was buried on McNeil Island. John's body was moved on 8 Apr 1938 to Trinity Lutheran Cemetery in Parkland, Pierce, Washington. His father was T Finwick. He was a warehouseman and farmer. John Finwick became a citizen of the United States on 10 Mar 1906.

20. **Floyd, Catherine J**: born 20 Jun 1839 in Clinton, Ohio. She died on 14 Apr 1919 in Meridian, Pierce, Washington and was buried on 18 Apr 1919 on McNeil Island. Catherine's body was moved on 10 Apr 1938 to Trinity Lutheran Cemetery in Parkland, Pierce, Washington. Her father was Eri Lamb and Rebecca Pearson. She was married to William Floyd.

21. **Floyd, Joseph Ery**: born 13 Dec 1861 in Sabina, Clinton, Ohio. He died 25 June 1935 in Meridian, Pierce, Washington and was buried on 26 June 1935 on McNeil Island. Joseph's body was moved on 10 Apr 1938 to Trinity Lutheran Cemetery in Parkland, Pierce, Washington. His parents are William Floyd and Cathrine Lamb. His wife was Mary Alice Leighton.

22. **Floyd, Mary Alice**: born 7 June 1854 in Tunkhannock, Wyoming, Pennsylvania. She died 16 Apr 1916 in Gertrude, Pierce, Washington and was buried on 18 April 1916 on McNeil Island. Mary's body was moved on 10 Apr 1938 to Trinity Lutheran Cemetery in Parkland, Pierce, Washington, Her parents are George Guthrie Leighton and Phoebe Gardner. Her husband was Joseph Ery Floyd.

23. **Floyd, William G**: born 11 Dec 1831 in Clinton, Ohio. He died 23 Aug 1907 and was buried in 1907 onMcNeil Island, Pierce, Washington. William's body was moved 10 Apr 1938 to Trinity Lutheran Cemetery in Parkland, Pierce, Washington. His wife was Cathrine J Lamb.

24. **Halverson, Gusta**: born in May 1894. She died 1907 and was buried on McNeil Island. Gusta's body was moved on 7 June 1937 to Trinity Lutheran Cemetery in Parkland, Pierce, Washington. Her parents are Andrew and Annie Halverson.

25. **Halverson, Mary Ellen**: born 2 July 1899 in Washington. She died on 24 Feb 1910 in Gertrude, McNeil Island, Pierce, Washington and was buried on 26 Feb 1910 on McNeil Island. Mary's body was moved on 7 June 1937 to Trinity Lutheran Cemetery in Parkland, Pierce, Washington. Her parents are Andrew and Annie Halverson. The death certificate says that she was an idiot, can't walk or talk.

26. **Halverson, Ole**: born 14 Apr 1855 in Norway. He died 12 Dec 1933 in Meridian, Pierce, Washington and was buried on 14 Dec 1933 on McNeil Island. Ole's body was moved on 26 Aug 1937 to Trinity Lutheran Cemetery in Parkland, Pierce, Washington. His wife in Julia Christianson

27. **Hannem, Bernt Bersvein Norman**: born 30 Apr 1855 in Tingvoll, More og Romsdal Norway. He died 30 Jan 1930 in Gertrude, McNeil Island, Pierce, Washington and was buried on 2 Feb 1930 on McNeil Island. Bernt's body was moved 15 Jun 1937 to Woodbine Cemetery in Puyallup, Pierce, Washington. His father was Nels Hannem. His wife was Bertha Hendrickson.

28. **Hanson, Olof Aaron**: born 12 Apr 1848 in Flaterud, Tisselskog, Älvsborg, Sweden. He died on 23 Aug 1934 in Tacoma, Pierce, Washington and was buried on 4 Sep 1934 on McNeil Island. Aaron's body was moved 8 Apr 1938 to Trinity Lutheran Cemetery in Parkland, Pierce, Washington. His parents are Hans Olofson and Anna Lisa Andersdotter. He immigrated to the United States in 1878 and was naturalized on 26 Oct 1892.

29. **Hanson, Johan August**: born 10 Feb 1855 in Flaterud, Tisselskog, Älvsborg, Sweden. He died 23 Oct 1917 in Tacoma, Pierce, Washington and was buried on 29 Oct 1917 on McNeil Island, John's body was moved on 8 Apr 1938 to Trinity Lutheran Cemetery in Parkland, Pierce, Washington, His parents are Hans Olofson and Anna Lisa Andersdotter.

30. **Harrison, Ralph**: 21 Jan 1864 in Pittsburg, Allegheny, Pennsylvania. He died 12 Oct 1920 in Gertrude, McNeil Island, Pierce, Washington and was buried on 15 Oct 1920 on McNeil Island. Ralph's body was moved on 3 Aug 1937 to New Tacoma Cemetery in University Place, Pierce, Washington, His parents are Ralph Harrison and Mary Cartledge. His wife was Carrie Virginia Uhrich Welsh. He was a carpenter.

31. **Hildinger, Madge F**: born 16 Oct 1875 in Piatt, Illinois. She died 30 May 1913 in Meridian, Pierce, Washington and was buried 1 June 1913 on McNeil Island. Madge's body was moved

on 2 Mar 1938 to Trinity Lutheran Cemetery in Parkland, Pierce, Washington. Her parents are Hiram Smock and Ann L Barnes. She was married on 8 Nov 1893 in Piatt Illinois to William Casper Hildinger.

32. **Holm, John**: born Oct 1847 in Sweden, He died 2 Sep 1930 in Tacoma, Pierce, Washington and was buried on McNeil Island. John's body was moved on 2 Jun 1937 to Tacoma, Pierce, Washington. His parents are Alexander Sjoholm and Anna Katrina Johansdatter. His wife was Petra Marie Nielsdatter. Birth name was Johannes Alexandersson. Immigrated in 1881.

33. **Iverson, Edward:** born 1855 in Sweden. He died 20 Oct 1907 on McNeil Island and was buried on McNeil Island. Edward's body was moved on 20 Dec 1937 to New Tacoma Cemetery in University Place, Pierce, Washington.

34. **Jansen, Isador Carl**: born 7 Jun 1885 in Hamre, Forsa, Gavleberg, Sweden. He died 21 Oct 1918 in Tacoma, Pierce, Washington and was buried on 26 Oct 1918 on McNeil Island. Isedor's body was moved on 24 May 1937 to Trinity Lutheran Cemetery in Parkland, Pierce, Washington. His parents are Carl Janson and Anna Sjoberg. His wife was Dora Sophia Christensen. He was a ship worker. He immigrated to the United State on 17 June 1903. He became a citizen on 30 Sep 1912. He had a light complexion. He was 5 feet 10 inches and weighed 175 lbs. He had light brown hair and blue eyes.

35. **Johnson, C Ludvig**: born 5 Oct 1863 in Sweden. He died 13 Dec 1921 on McNeil Island and was buried on 15 Dec 1921 on McNeil Island. Ludwig's body was moved on 17 Aug 1937 to Trinity Lutheran Cemetery in Parkland, Pierce, Washington. His father was Hans Nelson. His wife was Alma V.

36. **Johnson, Claus A**: born 1854 in Sweden. He died 2 Dec 1930 in Midland, Pierce, Washington and was buried on 6 Dec 1930 on McNeil Island. Claus's body was moved on 17 Aug 1937 to Trinity Lutheran Cemetery in Parkland, Pierce, Washington. His parents are Johannes Nelson and Mary Ann. His wife is Hanna.

37. **Jorgenson, Julius Andrew**: born 6 Dec 1854 in Norway.He died 20 Jun 1919 in Meridian, Pierce, Washington and buried on 22 Jun 1919 on McNeil Island. Julius's body was moved in Apr 1938 to Trinity Lutheran Cemetery in Parkland, Pierce, Washington. His father is Elling Jorgenson.

38. **Julin, Carl Johan**: born 8 Dec 1838 in Jonstorp, Malmöhus, Sweden. He died 3 Apr 1923 in Gertrude, Pierce, Washington and was buried on 5 Apr 1923 on McNeil Island. Charles's body was moved on 20 Dec 1937 to New Tacoma Cemetery in University Place, Pierce, Washington. His wife was Ida Sophia Peterson. He was a merchant. He was known as Charles.

39. **Julin, Alfred Emmanuel**: born 1 Jan 1878 in Kansas. He died 12 Mar 1917 in Gertrude, Pierce, Washington and was buried on 15 Mar 1917 on McNeil Island. Charles's body was

moved on 20 Dec 1937 to New Tacoma Cemetery in University Place, Pierce, Washington. His parents are Charles Julin and Ida Sophia Peterson.

40. **Julin, Gustave Fredalph**: born 31 Oct 1893 in Gertrude, Pierce, Washington. He died 13 Sep 1932 in Tacoma, Pierce, Washington and was buried on McNeil Island. Gustave's body was moved on 20 Dec 1937 to New Tacoma Cemetery in University Place, Pierce, Washington. His Parents are Charles Julin and Ida Sophia Peterson. He was short with medium build. He has blue eyes and light hair. His World War I draft card said he had physical disabilities and had to support his parents on the farm.

41. **Julin, Ida Sophia**: born 23 Oct 1859 in Vimmerby, Kalmar, Sweden. She died 11 Feb 1936 in Gertrude, Pierce, Washington and was buried on 15 Feb 1936 on McNeil Island. Ida's body was moved on 20 Dec 1937 to New Tacoma Cemetery in University Place, Pierce, Washington. Her father was Nels Peterson. Her husband was Charles Julin.

42. **Julin, Blenda Emelia Esther**: born 3 Nov 1879 in Kansas. She died 16 Apr 1925 in Tacoma, Pierce, Washington and was buried on 20 Apr 1925 on McNeil Island. Esther's body was moved on 20 Dec 1937 to New Tacoma Cemetery in University Place, Pierce, Washington. Her Parents are Charles Julin and Ida Sophia Peterson. She was a Postmaster.

43. **Kammen, Clara Isoline**: born 26 Oct 1887 in Fox Island, Pierce, Washington Territory. She died 21 Jun 1907 in Washington and was buried on McNeil Island. Clara's body was moved on 20 Aug 1937 to Trinity Lutheran Cemetery in Parkland, Pierce, Washington. Her parents are Hans Olsen Kammen and Inger Maria Johnsdatter Dyrud.

44. **Kammen, Inga Marie**: born 15 Nov 1856 in Stange, Østre Toten kommune, Oppland fylke, Norway. She died 29 Jan 1923 in Tacoma, Pierce, Washington and was buried on 2 Feb 1923 on McNeil Island. Enger's body was moved on 20 Aug 1937 to Trinity Lutheran Cemetery in Parkland, Pierce, Washington. Her father was John Johnson. Also known as Enger Marie Kammen.

45. **Kammen, Hans Olson**: born 2 Feb 1839 in Norway. He died 6 Sep 1908 in McNeil Island, Pierce, Washington and was buried on 8 Sep 1908 on McNeil Island. Hans's body was moved on 20 Aug 1937 to Trinity Lutheran Cemetery in Parkland, Pierce, Washington. His wife was Enger Marie Johnsdatter Dyrud.

46. **Knutson, Gertrude**: 24 Jan 1846 in Norway. She died 29 Sep 1931 on McNeil Island, Pierce, Washington and was buried on 1 Oct 1931 on McNeil Island. Gertrude's body was moved in Apr 1938 to Trinity Lutheran Cemetery in Parkland, Pierce, Washington. Her parents are Johan Strand and Olova Rawstad. Her husband was Peter Knutson.

47. **Larson, Andrew G**: born 1837 in Sweden. He died 3 Nov 1907 in Tacoma, Pierce, Washington and was buried 8 Nov 1907 on McNeil Island. Andrew's body was moved on 17 Aug 1937 to New Tacoma Cemetery in University Place, Pierce, Washington.

48. **Larson, Harold M**: born 8 Dec 1894 in Tacoma, Pierce, Washington. He died 15 Jun 1911 in Tacoma, Pierce, Washington and was buried on 16 Jun 1911 in Gertrude, McNeil Island, Pierce, Washington. Harold's body was moved on 25 Feb 1938 to Tacoma Cemetery in Tacoma, Pierce, Washington. His parents are Martin Larson and Minnie Neilson.

49. **McCaughan, Daniel P**: born 6 Jun 1859 in Abbey, Renfrewshire, Scotland. He died 21 May 1928 on McNeil Island, Pierce, Washington and was buried on 23 May 1928 on McNeil Island. Daniel's body was moved on 16 Jun 1937 to Mt View Cemetery in Tacoma, Pierce, Washington, His parents are Archibald McCaughan and Margaret Watt. His wife is Clara Belle . He was a rancher. His son Wilbur served in the US Marines in China.

50. **Michaelson, Elizabeth Kataline**: born 9 Jul 1872 in Minnesota, She died 1 April 1916 in Gertrude, Pierce, Washington and buried on 3 Apr 1916 on McNeil Island, Elizabeth's body was moved on 18 Aug 1937 to Trinity Lutheran Cemetery in Parkland, Pierce, Washington. Her father H O Kammen. Her husband was Henry Michaelson.

51. **Michaelson, Helen**: She died in 1906 and was buried on McNeil Island. Helen's body was moved on 18 Aug 1937 to Trinity Lutheran Cemetery in Parkland, Pierce, Washington. Her parents are Henry Michaelson and Elizabeth Kataline Kammen.

52. **Michaelson, Oscar Harry**: born 2 April 1899 in Wisconsin. He died 15 July 1915 in Tacoma, Pierce, Washington and was buried on 18 April 1915 on McNeil Island. Oscar's body was moved on 18 Aug 1937 to Trinity Lutheran Cemetery in Parkland, Pierce, Washington. His parents are Henry Michaelson and Elizabeth Kataline Kammen.

53. **Moard, Charles**: born 29 Mar 1850 in Sweden. He died 14 Feb 1923 on McNeil Island, Pierce, Washington and was buried on 19 Feb 1923 on McNeil Island. Charles's body was moved on 12 Apr 1937 to Tacoma Cemetery in Tacoma, Pierce, Washington. His father is Andrew A Moard. His wife is Nellie Johnson

54. **Nelson, George A**: born 1 Jan 1846 in Sweden. He died 16 Oct 1927 in Tacoma, Pierce, Washington and was buried on 18 Oct 1927 on McNeil Island. George's body was moved in Apr 1938 to Trinity Lutheran Cemetery in Parkland, Pierce, Washington. His parents are Andrew Nelson and Emma. He was a painter.

55. **Nelson, Hermikka Nicolia**: born 5 Feb 1876 in Bergen, Norway. She died 15 May 1923 in Tacoma, Pierce, Washington and was buried on 19 May 1923 on McNeil Island. Hermikka's body was moved 2 Jun 1937 to Tacoma Cemetery in Tacoma, Pierce, Washington. Her parents are Niels Peter Nielson and Hermikke Lovise Fredrikke Sorensdatter.

56. **Nelson, Olivia**: born 10 December 1864 in Hoganas, Malmohus, Sweden. She died 12 January 1930 on McNeil Island, Pierce, Washington and was buried on 14 January 1930 on McNeil Island. Her parents are Nils Pulson and Bolinda Lundblad. Her husband was Gustaf Nelson. When Gustaf died in 1932 he was buried in New Tacoma Cemetery in Tacoma, Pierce Her body was moved to New Tacoma Cemetery, University Place, Pierce, Washington in 1937 or 1938.

57. **Norris, John N**: born 17 Mar 1860 in Illinois. He died 17 Feb 1922 on McNeil Island, Pierce, Washington and was buried on 19 May 1922 on McNeil Island. His wife is Maria. He was a miner.

58. **Nyberg, Anna Amanda**: born 24 June 1884 in Kansas. She died 19 Nov 1918 in Fort Steilacoom, Pierce, Washington and was buried on 20 Nov 1918 on McNeil Island. Anna's body was moved on 16 June 1937 toTrinity Lutheran Cemetery in Parkland, Pierce, Washington. Her Parents are Erick Nyberg and Martha. Her husband was Felix Benrobters.

59. **Nyberg, Erick Eriksson**: born 8 Nov 1856 in Alfta, Gavleborg, Sweden. He died 10 Oct 1935 in Seattle, King, Washington and was buried on 13 Oct 1935 on McNeil Island. Erick's was moved on 16 Jun 1937 to Trinity Lutheran Cemetery in Parkland, Pierce, Washington. He was married to Martha Augusta Soderstrom in 1880.

60. **Nyberg, Martha Augusta**: born 15 Jun 1855 in Sweden. She died 22 Nov 1922 in Gertrude, Pierce, Washington and was buried on 25 Nov 1922 on McNeil Island. Martha's body was moved 16 Jun 1937 to Trinity Lutheran Cemetery in Parkland, Pierce, Washington. Her Parents are Anders Gustaf Soderstrom and Margreta "Martha" Andersdotter. She was married on 12 July 1880 in Alfta, Gavleborg, Sweden to Erick Eriksson Nyberg.

61. **Nyman, Carl G**: born 4 Apr 1858 in Sweden. He died 9 Jun 1925 in Gertrude, Pierce, Washington and was buried on 13 Jun 1925 on McNeil Island. Carl's body was moved 8 Apr 1938 to Trinity Lutheran Cemetery in Parkland, Pierce, Washington, He married on 12 Apr 1902 in Pierce, Washington to Erika Larson.

62. **Nyman, Erika**: born 23 Mar 1863 in Sweden. She died 29 Jul 1917 in Gertrude, Pierce, Washington and was buried on 1 Aug 1917 on McNeil Island. Erika's body was moved on 8 Apr 1938 to Trinity Lutheran Cemetery in Parkland, Pierce, Washington, She married on 12 Apr 1902 in Pierce, Washington to Carl Nyman. Her maiden name was Larson. She immigrated to the United States in 1872;

63. **Upsal, Peter L** : born 1852 in Norway. He died on 5 Jan 1928 in Tacoma, Pierce, Washington and was buried on Meridian, McNeil Island, Pierce, Washington. Peter's body was moved in Apr 1938 to Trinity Lutheran Cemetery in Parkland, Pierce, Washington. He was a carpenter. Death certificate has Upsal and Disinterment Permit has Opsahl.

64. **Parr, Irene Marie**: born 23 Feb 1918 in Meridian, Pierce, Washington. She died 13 Mar 1918 in Meridian, Pierce, Washington and was buried on 15 Mar 1918 on McNeil Island. Irene's body was moved in Apr 1938 to Trinity Lutheran Cemetery in Parkland, Pierce, Washington. Her parents are Fred Willis Parr and Selma Irene Taylor. Listed on Disinterment Permit is infant Parr.

65. **Paul, Leone**: born 28 Feb 1922 in Washington. She died 14 Mar 1922 in Gertrude, Pierce, Washington and was buried on 15 Mar 1922 on McNeil Island. Leona's body was moved on 8 Apr 1938 to Trinity Lutheran Cemetery in Parkland, Pierce, Washington. Her parents are John Wesley Paul and Katherine Hazel Burbank.

66. **Pearson, Lilli**: born 7 Sep 1884 in Hoganas, Malmohus, Sweden. She died 5 Feb 1920 in Gertrude, Pierce, Washington and was buried on 9 Feb 1920 on McNeil Island. Lilli's body was moved 10 Aug 1937 to New Tacoma Cemetery in University Place, Pierce, Washington. Her parents are Alfred Johanson and Tilda Nelson, Her husband was Leander Pearson.

67. **Peterson, Hokan**: born 11 Jul 1832 in Sweden. He died 8 Jan 1920 at Fort Steilacoom, Pierce, Washington and was buried on McNeil Island. Hokan's body was moved on 2 Jun 1937 to Trinity Lutheran Cemetery in Parkland, Pierce, Washington. His father is Peter.

68. **Seagrave, Ellen Sophia**: born 8 Mar 1857 in Sterling, Cayuga, New York. She died 16 Aug 1913 in Seattle,King, Washington and was buried on McNeil Island. Ella's body was moved 2 Mar 1938 to Trinity Lutheran Cemetery in Parkland, Pierce, Washington, Her parents are John Pettis and Hattie Green. She married on 2 Apr 1879 in Crawford, Iowa to Herbert Newton Seagrave.

69. **Seagrave, Herbert Newton**: born 22 Dec 1851 in Sturbridge, Worcester, Massachusetts. He died 10 Sep 1914 in Steilacoom, Pierce, Washington and was buried on McNeil Island. Herbert's body was moved 2 Mar 1938 to Trinity Lutheran Cemetery in Parkland, Pierce, Washington. He married on 2 Apr 1879 to Ellen Sophia Pettis.

70. **Seagrave**: He died and was buried 1910 on McNeil Island. This boy's body was moved on 2 Mar 1938 to Trinity Lutheran Cemetery in Parkland, Pierce, Washington.

71. **Sherman, Elmer Grant**: born 15 Nov 1862 in Illinois. He died 15 Jan 1914 in Still Harbor. Pierce, Washington and was buried on 17 Jan 1914 on McNeil Island. Elmer's body was moved in Apr 1938 to Trinity Lutheran Cemetery in Parkland, Pierce, Washington. His parents are Samuel Dennis Sherman and Margaret A Pason . His wife is Martha Annetta Luzader. He was a carpenter.

72. **Sherman, Gaylord Luzader**: born 15 Dec 1899 in Washington. He died 28 Apr 1919 in Tacoma, Pierce, Washington and was buried on 1 May 1919 on McNeil Island. Gaylord's body was moved in Apr 1938 to Trinity Lutheran Cemetery in Parkland, Pierce, Washington, His parents are Elmer Grant Sherman and Martha Annetta Luzader. His WWI draft card says he

was a teamster. He was tall, slender, with brown hair and brown eyes. It says he had weak lungs and ankles.

73. **Seaburg, Marie**: born 5 Nov 1829 in Värmlands län, Gavleborg, Sweden. She died 6 Sep 1908 in Gertrude, Pierce, Washington and was buried 1908 on McNeil Island. Marie's body was moved 24 May 1937 to Trinity Lutheran Cemetery in Parkland, Pierce, Washington. Her maiden name is Svensdotter. Her husband was Olaf Nilsson. Listed on Disinterment Permit as Marie Sjoberg

74. **Steen, Christian S**: born 12 Oct 1856 in Norway. He died 6 Jan 1921 and was buried Jan 1921 on McNeil Island. Christain's body was moved 29 Aug 1937 to Trinity Lutheran Cemetery in Parkland, Pierce, Washington.

75. **Tangen, Carl Oswald**: born 19 July 1887 in Minnesota. He died 23 Nov 1905 in Olympia, Thruston, Washington and was buried on 27 Nov 1905 on McNeil Island. Carl's body was moved on 27 May 1937 to Trinity Lutheran Cemetery in Parkland, Pierce, Washington. HIs parents are Carl G Tangen and Emma Seaberg.

76. **Tangen, Christian**: born 7 July 1852. He died 9 Oct 1905 and was buried 1905 on McNeil Island. Chris's body was moved to Trinity Lutheran Cemetery in Parkland, Pierce, Washington.

77. **Tangen, Emma**: born 19 Jan 1861 in Sweden. She died 5 Oct 1916 on McNeil Island, Pierce, Washington and was buried on 8 Oct 1916 on McNeil Island. Emma's body was moved 27 May 1937 to Trinity, Pierce, Washington. Her maiden name is Seaberg, Her husband is Carl G Tangen.

78. **Tangen**: died 1905 and was buried on McNeil Island. This baby's body was moved 25 Feb 1938 to Trinity Lutheran Cemetery in Parkland, Pierce, Washington.

79. **Tangen**: this baby's body was moved 27 May 1937.

80. **Ward, James Samuel**: born Aug 1858 In Illinois. He died 3 Nov 1917 in Bee, Pierce, Washington and was buried on 6 nov 1917 on McNeil Island. James's body was moved Apr 1938 to Trinity Lutheran Cemetery in Parkland, Pierce, Washington. His father is Jas S Ward. His wife is Caroline Christine Schubert. He was a Postmaster.

81. **Wedman, Anna Lovise**: born 17 Feb 1877 in Sweden. She died 21 May 1921 on Lakeview, Pierce, Washington in Mountain View Sanatorium, and was buried 28 May 1921 on McNeil Island. Anna's body was moved 2 Jun 1937 to Trinity Lutheran Cemetery in Parkland, Pierce, Washington. Her parents are Peter Eric Ramstedt and Catherine. Her husband is Otto Edward Wedman.

82. **Wedman, Clarence Frederick**: born 14 Apr 1902 in Milwaukee, Milwaukee, Wisconsin. He died 18 Feb 1925 in Tacoma, Pierce, Washington and was buried 1925 on McNeil Island. Clarence's body was moved 2 Jun 1937 to Trinity Lutheran Cemetery in Parkland, Pierce, Washington. His parents are Otto Edward Wedman and Anna Lovisa Ramstedt.

83. **Westman, Daniel**: born 8 Oct 1849 in Sweden. He died 10 Aug 1929 in Gertrude, Pierce, Washington and was buried on 15 Aug 1929 on McNeil Island. Daniel's body was moved 26 June 1937 to Puyallup Cemetery in Puyallup, Pierce, Washington according to the Disinterment Permit, but to Trinity Lutheran Cemetery according to Find-a grave. His wife is Eva Johanna Johanson. He was a Carpenter.

84. **Westman, Eva Johanna**: born 22 Apr 1849 in Sweden. She died 27 Apr 1934 Gertrude, Pierce, Washington and was buried on 2 May 1934 on McNeil Island. Eva's body was moved 16 Jun 1937 to Puyallup Cemetery in Puyallup, Pierce, Washington according to the Disinterment Permit, but to Trinity Lutheran Cemetery according to Find-a grave. Her maiden name was Johanson. She was married to Daniel Westman.

85. **Westman, baby girl**: born 31 Oct 1915 in Washington. She died 31 Oct 1915 Gertrude, Pierce, Washington and was buried on 1 Nov 1915 on McNeil Island. Her body was moved 16 Jun 1937. Her parents are Walfred O Westman and Wilhelmina Nyberg.

86. **Williams, Emilie Margaret**: born 24 Mar 1894 in Boston, Massachusetts. She died 11 Jun 1928 on McNeil Island, Pierce, Washington and was buried on 13 Jun 1928 McNeil Island. Emilie's body was moved on 22 Oct 1928. Her parents are William Collins and Mary Ann. Her husband is Frank Klayton Williams.

87. **Winters, Vella**: born 15 May 1906 in Washington, She died 21 Jun 1911 in Meridian, Pierce, Washington and was buried on 23 Jun 1911 on McNeil Island. Vella's body was moved 10 Apr 1938 to Trinity Lutheran Cemetery in Parkland, Pierce, Washington. Her parents are Lawrence Winters and Nancy AdelaideFloyd.

88. **Wolfe, baby girl**: born 15 Dec 1913 Pierce, Washington. She died 15 Dec 1913 in Still Harbor, McNeil Island, Pierce, Washington and was buried on McNeil Island. Her body was moved to Trinity Lutheran Cemetery in Parkland, Pierce, Washington. Her parents are George M Wolfe and Dollie Smith.

There were 21 people buried in the prisoners cemetery next to the US Penitentiary and were removed in 1904 to the current prisoners cemetery. The current cemetery has 143 prisoners buried there. The first 125 graves are marked with numbered graves from 1 to 125. The other 18 have gravestones with their names, birth dates and death dates from 1961 to 1972. After 1972 it was decided to bury prisoners off the island. These prisoners were ones that the families were not known to the prison or who couldn't afford to pay to have the body removed for them to send home for burial.

1. **Name: Levi Livingston**
    Conviction: counterfeiting in Washington State
    Sentenced: Sept 1878 for 5 years
    Died; Apr 1879 on McNeil Island, Pierce, Washington

    Levi grew up in King County Washington, He got involved with a gang of counterfers in Oregon. He barely escaped going to jail at that time and came back to Washington, but he continued in crime where he was sent to McNeil Island. Levi was well known as a common thief in the area. After nearly going to jail in Oregon, he came back to Washington. There he married a respectable widow and then he got hired at a logging camp. When he was arrested for counterfeiting half dollar coins, his wife was so willing to tell the police all that she knew.

2. **Name: Ah Isau** 223
    Sentenced: deportation to China
    Discharge for good behavior: deported 2 October 1890
    Born: 1855 in China
    Age when imprisoned: 35
    Height: 5 foot 11 inches
    Weight: 140
    Hair: black
    Eyes: black
    Occupation: laborer
    Died: 10 May 1890 on McNeil Island, Pierce, Washington

3. **Name: A J Fletcher** 349
    Conviction: Selling Liquor to Indians
    Sentenced: 6 months
    Born: 1828
    Age when imprisoned: 62
    Height: 5 foot 10 inches
    Weight: 170 lbs
    Hair: light

Complexion: old gray beard
Eyes: blue
Died: 17 October 1890 on McNeil Island, Pierce, Washington

4. **Name: Katz Kay-ish** 42
    Conviction: manslaughter
    Sentenced: 8 September 1886 for 10 years and $1000 fine
    Born: 1828
    Age when imprisoned: 58
    Height: 5 foot 8 inches
    Weight: 160
    Hair: none
    Eyes: black
    Died: 24 June 1891 on McNeil Island, Pierce, Washington

5. **Name: Tom Kook-ish** 242
    Conviction: perjury
    Sentenced:7 January 1888 for 5 years
    Discharge for good behavior:
    Born: 1855 in Alaska
    Age when imprisoned: 33
    Height: 5 foot 7 inches
    Weight: 160
    Hair: black
    Eyes: black
    Died: 25 June 1891 on McNeil Island, Pierce, Washington

6. **Name: Ah Yow** 490
    Conviction: Violation Res. Act
    Arrested/Trial: Seattle, Washington/same
    Sentenced: 28 January 1892 for deportation to China
    Born: 1863 in China
    Age when imprisoned: 25
    Height: 5 foot 5 inches
    Weight: 145
    Hair: black
    Eyes: black
    Occupation: laborer
    Died: 12 February 1892 on McNeil Island, Pierce, Washington
7. **Name: Samuel Hays** 440 42
    Alias: Martin Burrett
    Conviction: selling liquor to Indians

Arrested/Trail:Yakima, Washington/Walla Walla, Washington
Sentenced: 1 November 1892
Plead: not guilty
Discharge for good behavior: 25 August 1893
Born: 1859 in San Francisco, California
Age when imprisoned: 33
Marital Status: single
Able to read: yes
Able to write: yes
Height: 5 foot 8 inches
Weight: 140 lbs
Hair: light brown
Complexion: fair
Eyes: Gray
Occupation: Blacksmith
Died: 4 February 1893 on McNeil Island, Pierce, Washington from heart failure

8. **Name: Chas Carlson**, 684 440
   Alias : Chas Nelson
   Conviction: Selling liquor to the Indians Yakima, Washington
   Arrested/Trail: Yakima, Washington/Walla Walla, Washington
   Sentenced: 15 November 1894 for 8 months
   Plead: guilty
   Discharge for good behavior: 5 July 1895
   Born: 1846 in Sweden
   Age when imprisoned: 48
   Marital Status: single
   Able to read: a little
   Able to write: no
   Height: 5 foot 7 inches
   Weight: 150
   Hair: bald light brown
   Complexion: fair
   Eyes: light blue
   Occupation: farm labor
   Died: 18 February 1895 on McNeil Island, Pierce, Washington from suicide

9. **Name: Ed Hanson**
   Alias: E H Lasken
   Conviction: Counterfeiting in Spokane County, Washington
   Sentenced: 19 April 1901 for 10 years
   Discharge for good behavior: 26 September 1909
   Born: 1846 in Wisconsin

Age when imprisoned: 55
Marital Status: married
Able to read: yes
Able to write: yes
Height: 5 foot 7 ¾ inches
Weight: 148 ½ lbs
Hair: gray
Complexion: fair
Eyes: light blue
Occupation: farmer
Died: 23 September 1902 on McNeil Island, Pierce, Washington from gunshot wound from the day before.

Ed Hanson was the last of a gang of counterfeiters to be sentenced for their crime. They had been the most successful in the Spokane area, but now businesses can rest a little easier.

10.   **Name: George A Sanborn**
Conviction: Selling liquor to Indians in Anacortes, Washington
Sentenced: 24 Dec 1901 for 2 years and $100 fine and costs
Discharge for good behavior: 25 September 1903
Born: 1841 New Hampshire
Age when imprisoned: 60
Marital Status: married
Able to read: yes
Able to write: yes
Height: 5 foot 9 ¾ inches
Weight: 146 lbs
Hair: black and gray
Complexion: fair
Eyes: hazel
Occupation: carpenter
Died: 1 May 1903 on McNeil Island, Pierce, Washington

11.   **Name: Erick Lintula**
Conviction: cutting and stabbing with intent to kill in Douglas, Alaska
Sentenced: 26 December 1902 for 2 ½ years
Plead: guilty
Discharge for good behavior: 28 December 1904
Born: 1856 in Finland
Age when imprisoned: 46
Marital Status: single
Able to read: no
Able to write: no

Height: 5 foot 9 ¾ inches
Weight: 144
Hair: light
Complexion: fair
Eyes: blue
Occupation: miner
Died: 3 May 1904 in McNeil Island, Pierce, Washington

12.   **Name: Nephi Ohpel**
Conviction: Assault with intent to kill in Pocatello, Idaho
Sentenced: 17 April 1902 for 2 ½ years
Plead: not guilty
Discharge for good behavior: 20 May 1904
Born: 1852 in Fort Hall, Bingham, Idaho
Age when imprisoned: 50
Marital Status: married
Able to read: no
Able to write: no
Height: 5 foot 8 ½ inches
Weight: 163 lbs
Hair:
Complexion: dark
Eyes: black
Occupation: rancher
Died: 11 September 1903 on McNeil Island, Pierce, Washington

13.   **Name: Jim Kishtoo**
Conviction: Murder in 2nd degree in , Pyramid Harbor, Alaska
Sentenced: 27 June 1900 for 50 years
Discharge for good behavior: 9 April 1942
Born:1855 in Klukwan, Haines Borough, Alaska
Age when imprisoned: 45
Marital Status: married
Able to read: no
Able to write: no
Height: 5 foot 5 ½ inches
Weight:155
Hair: Black
Complexion:Medium for Indian
Eyes: Black
Died:19 November 1905 on McNeil Island, Pierce. Washington

Jim was arrested with 5 other people for the death of a couple. You can read the story under James Hanson. He was the leader of the group.

14. **Name: Mark Clanat**
Conviction: murder in 2nd degree in Chileah, Alaska
Sentenced: 27 June 1900 for 20 years
Discharge for good behavior: 26 February 1917
Born: 1864 in Chilkat, Haines Borough, Alaska
Age when imprisoned: 36
Marital Status: married
Able to read: yes
Able to write: yes
Height: 5 foot 7 inches
Weight: 150
Hair: black
Complexion: light shallow
Eyes: small black
Occupation:
Died: 7 March 1904 on McNeil Island, Pierce, Washington from Tuberculosis

Mark was arrested with 5 other people for the death of a couple. You can read the story under James Hanson. He was the leader of the group.

15. **Name: F Barrett**
Conviction: Violation in Montpelier, Idaho
Sentenced: 15 April 1903 for 10 years and $100 fine
Plead: not guilty
Discharge for good behavior: 14 January 1910
Born: 1852 Scotland
Age when imprisoned: 49
Marital Status: single
Able to read: yes
Able to write: yes
Height: 5 foot 8 ½ inches
Weight: 132 ½ lbs
Hair: gray
Complexion: light
Eyes: gray blue
Occupation: laborer
Died: 3 April 1905 on McNeil Island, Pierce, Washington

16. **Name: Fraun Richards**
English for Fraun is Frank

Conviction: Counterfeiting in Seattle, King, Washington
Sentenced: 21 June 1905 for 5 years and $100 fine
Plead: guilty
Discharge for good behavior: 22 March 1909
Born: 1859 in Seattle, King, Washington
Age when imprisoned: 46
Marital Status: single
Able to read: yes
Able to write: yes
Height: 5 foot 7 ½ inches
Weight: 123
Hair: black or dark brown
Complexion: fair
Eyes: Hazel
Occupation: teamster
Died: 27 June 1905 on McNeil Island, Pierce, Washington from suicied by morphine .

Frank Richards, who was born Fraun Richards, died only six days after going to McNeil Island to serve his sentence. He had previously served a five years sentence in the Walla Walla penitentiary for robbery and had been released just one month before being arrested for manufacturing counterfeit coins. He pleaded guilty to manufacturing counterfeit coins. The prison officials were surprised at his death. He had been at the prison only 6 days and looked to be in good health. That day he died the work assigned to him cheerfully with no complaints of illness. When he was arrested. The secret service officers found him melting metal over a fire to then pour it into molds nearby. Richards took all the blame, saving his sister and brother-in-law from prosecution. Richards had been in prison before for robbery and was a member of a gang of criminals. It was first thought that his death was from heart disease, but an autopsy showed he had a dose of morphine.

17. **Name: Benjamin Koh-suk-dake** (TDL 14 AUG 1905 p. 5 DIES IN PRISON)
Conviction: Manslaughter in Juniah, Alaska
Sentenced: 31 Dec 1901 for 4 years
Plead: guilty.
Discharge for good behavior: Jan 25 1906
Born:1877 in Hoonah, Alaska
Age when imprisoned:24
Marital Status: single
Able to read: no
Able to write: no
Height: 5 foot 6 3/4 inches
Weight: 160 lbs.
Hair: black.
Complexion: Indian

Eyes: dark brown.
Occupation: laborer.
Died:12 Aug 1905 on McNeil Island, Pierce, Washington from Tuberculosis

18. **Name: Jim Hanson**
Conviction: Murder 1st degree in Skagway, Alaska
Sentenced: 28 May 1900 to be hung, which was changed in Nov 1900 to life in prison.
Plead: guilty
Discharged for good behavior: Life
Born: 1876 in Alaska.
Age when imprisoned: 25 years and 10 Months
Marital Status: married
Able to read: No
Able to write: No
Height: 5 foot 9 inches
Weight: 180 lbs
Hair: black
Complexion: medium for Indian
Eyes: black
Occupation: hunter and trapper
Died: 13 Aug 1905 on McNeil Island, Pierce, Washington

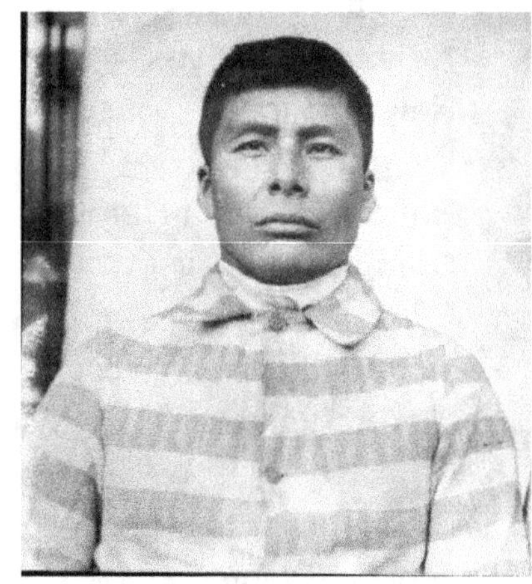

Jim Hanson is his English name, his native name was Qualth. He was the leader of the Kahk-won-tons tribe. Jim was known as a bear fighter, because he killed a bear with a knife as a teenager. He was a good hunter and was strong and healthy. This was why he was a leader at such a young age. This tribe and some of the Chilkats are getting together for an inter-tribal potlatch. Jim's brother, wife and son left in a canoe to visit other tribes to invite them to the potlatch and gather supplies for the feast. Their canoe was damaged and they were drowned in the river. Jim, his wife Martha, and 11 other family and friends got into a war canoe to look for them. They came across a young couple camping not far from where a pierce of the canoe was found. The couple said they had seen a canoe with three people a few days earlier. After talking it was decided that the couple had something to do with the three deaths so they must die. The group went to the camp. They left three at the canoe while the other 9 went ashore. They only saw the husband and while Mark Clanet talked to the husband Jim Hanson shot him in the heart. His wife came out of the tent and was shot two times by Kichton. Once in the face and once in the chest. Then Jim Williams, age 17, slit her throat to finish the job. The couple was Bert and Florence Horton; they started their camping trip around the 1st of October 1899. Around the 14th of March 1900, Jim had gone into Skagway. There he came across a Salvation Army meeting. As he listened he was impressed with the message and the man conducting the meeting. At the end of the meeting Jim confist to the murders of the Hortons. JIm was advised to turn himself in to the civil authorities. He did this knowing he was going to die. His trail was quick and he was sentenced of murder on 28th May 1900. Jim was sentenced 27 June 1900 and made this statement "Brother, you must do your duty. I want to die for my crime that my people may live: that they may see what religion can do, even for one so wicked as I. Let them see how a Christian can die, and maybe they will kill no more white people. Maybe the young men of my tribe will take warning, Maybe they will not drink so much, but will become soldiers in God's army as I have. I am ready to die. You can take my body and do as you like with it; you can't hurt that." He was sentenced to hang within the next 30 days. Judge Brown asked the Governor to postpone Qualth's sentence so that the Attorney General could write to the President to have the sentence reduced to life in prison. The Governor agreed. The letter was written and signed by the Attorney General, the Judge, a U S Marshall, the District Attorney, and a long list of citizens. President William McKinley commuted his sentence to life in prison on the 11th of November 1900. Jim was 25 at his trial and 29 when he died.

For their testimonies as witnesses 7 in the group were not indicted. They were John (age 14) Kitcktoo, James Quaniish, Paddy Unahootch, George White native namae Goos, Dave Klanat and Martha Hanson. The next trail was for Jim Williams he got murder 2nd degree and was sentenced for 50 years. Jim got out for good behavior in 1901 and died of Tuberculosis on 8th of May 1902 in Alaska. The same conviction was given to the rest of the group arrested. Mark Klanat (Clanet) was sentenced to 20 years and died on McNeil Island, Day Kanateen was sentenced to 30 years (he was at McNeil Island from 6th of July 1900 until 19th on October 1900 when he was sent to San Quentin Prison due to overcrowding), and Jim Kitchtoo (father to John Kitchtoo) was sentenced to 50 years and died on McNeil Island, and Juch Klane was sentenced to 22 years was a last one alive. His sentence was commuted to "time served" by President Taft and he was sent home on the 17th of June 1910. Officials credit his longevity with Tuberculosis to the fact he has an outdoor job,piloting the prison boat to and from McNeil Island. Officials say that Jim lived a christian life while in jail and brought christianity to 100 fellow prisoners.

19. **Name: Gabriel Plugak**

Conviction: Manslaughter in Muskoka, Alaska
Sentenced: 3 December 1903 for 4 years
Discharged for good behavior: 30 January 1907
Born: 1879
Age when Imprisoned: 24
Marital Status: married
Able to read: no
Able to write: no
Height: 5 foot 3 ¾ inches
Weight: 129
Hair: Black
Occupation: Fisherman
Died: 12 October 1906 on McNeil Island, Pierce, Washington

Gabriel was at the bar after work with many people from work. There were drunken brawls. Gabriel decided to end one with a shovel blade to the other person's forehead. He lived for two weeks and then Gabriel was arrested for murder. He pled guilty to manslaughter.

20. **Name**: **Esquimau Natirg Anosuk**
Conviction: Manslaughter in Point Clarence, Alaska
Sentenced: 2 September 1903 for 3 years
Plead: Guilty
Discharge for good behavior: 6 May 1907
Born: 1869 in St Clarence, Alaska
Age when imprisoned: 34
Marital Status: single
Able to read: no
Able to write: no
Height: 5 foot 5 ½ inches
Weight: 131 ½ lbs
Hair: Black
Complexion: Esquima
Eyes: Brown
Occupation: Whaler
Died: 4 February 1907 on McNeil Island, Pierce, Washington from Tuberculosis

21. **Name: John Buckley**
Conviction: Selling liquor to Indians in Douglas, Alaska
Sentenced: 26 August 1909 for 2 years
Plead: not guilty
Discharge for good behavior: 17 April 1911
Born: 1862 Australia
Age when imprisoned: 47
Marital Status: single
Able to read: yes
Able to write: yes
Height: 5 foot 5 ½ inches
Weight: 157 ½ lbs
Hair: black with gray
Complexion: dark
Eyes: brown
Occupation: marine fireman
Died: 27 Aug 1910 on McNeil Island, Pierce, Washington of Tuberculosis of throat

22. **Name: Assairuk**
Conviction: Selling and giving liquor to Indians in Nome, Alaska
Sentenced: 13 May 1910 for 1 year
Plead: Guilty
Discharge for good behavior: 18 March 1911
Born: 1880

Age when imprisoned: 31
Marital Status: married
Able to read: no
Able to write: no
Height: 5 foot 2 inches in shoes
Weight: 115
Hair: Black
Complexion: yellow
Eyes: Dark Brown
Occupation: Housewife
Died: 21 March 1911 on McNeil Island, Pierce, Washington from Tuberculosis

23. **Name: Simeon Sergine**
Conviction: Manslaughter in Sand Point, Alaska
Sentenced: 21 Dec 1904 for 20 years
Plead: not guilty
Discharged for good behavior: 15 July 1918
Born: Alaska
Age when imprisoned: 27
Marital Status: single
Able to read: no
Able to write: no
Height: 5 foot 1 ¼ inches
Weight: 136 lbs
Hair: gray
Complexion: Indian
Eyes: Hazel brown
Occupation: dairying, shoemaking
Died: 8 June 1911 on McNeil Island, Pierce, Washington from Tuberculosis of lungs

24. **Name: Lewis Turner**
Alias: Frank Burns
Conviction: Counterfeiting in Vancouver, Washington
Sentenced: 9 June 1908 for 7 years
Plead: guilty
Discharged for good behavior: 15 July 1918
Born: California
Age when imprisoned: 32
Marital Status: single
Able to read: yes
Able to write: ywa
Height: 5 foot 9 ⅛ inches
Weight: 148 ½ lbs

Hair: black
Complexion: fair
Eyes: dark brown
Occupation: miner
Died: 4 Aug 1911 on McNeil Island, Pierce, Washington from Pulmonary Tuberculosis

25. **Name: Mike George**
Conviction: Selling liquor to Indians in Elko, Nevada
Sentenced: 19 October 1911 for 1 year
Plead: Guilty
Discharge for good behavior: 7 September 1912
Born: September 1861 Austria
Age when imprisoned: 50
Marital Status: widower
Able to read: no
Able to write: no
Height: 5 foot 7 ¼ inches
Weight: 162 lbs
Hair: dark brown
Complexion: sallow
Eyes: brown
Occupation: corn laborer
Died: 21 March 1912 on McNeil Island, Pierce, Washington from Nephritis

26. **Name: Paul Clein**
Real name: Paul Kramsminsky
Conviction: Murder in Spokane, Washington
Sentenced: 22 May 1911 for natural life
Discharge for good behavior: natural life
Born: 20 January 1873 in Germany
Age when imprisoned: 38
Parents: Johan Clein
Marital Status: widower
Able to read: yes
Able to write: yes
Height: 5 foot 11 ⅛ inches
Weight: 173
Hair: brown
Complexion: Fair
Eyes: brown
Occupation: cabinet maker

Died: 20 May 1914 on McNeil Island, Pierce, Washington Cancer of the Stomach

Paul Killed a man whose last name Sadowsky was a cabinet maker. His fiancee Mrs. Ida May Douglas stood by Paul proclaiming his innocence. His attorneys filed a motion for a new trial and a motion for an arrest of judgment, because they say that the court and prosecuting attorney had no jurisdiction. They also claimed that the verdict was contrary to the law and the evidence. Paul was arrested for the murder of a Paul Lewandowski, who's boby was found on Fort Wright military reservation ina yellow, rubber-tired buggy.

27. **Name: Daniel Brownfield**
Conviction: Counterfeiting in San Francisco, California
Sentenced: 15 September 1913 for 3 years
Plead: not guilty
Discharge for good behavior: 10 January 1916
Born: 7 July 1883 Seattle, King, Washington
Age when imprisoned:30
Marital Status: widower
Parents: S M Brownfield
Able to read: yes
Able to write: yes
Height: 5 foot 4 ½ inches
Weight: 143
Hair: light brown
Complexion: fair
Eyes: blue-gray
Occupation: Sailor

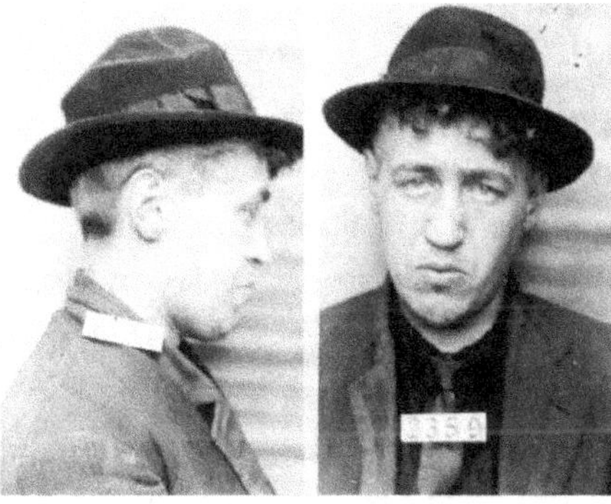

Died: 20 Oct 1914 on McNeil Island, Pierce, Washington from Paralysis and Malignant endocarditis

28. **Name: Horn Ging Lung**
Alias: Sam Wing
Conviction: Conspiracy in Oceanside, California
Sentenced: 2 January 1915 for 18 months
Plead: not guilty
Discharge for good behavior: 20 March 1916
Born: 1851 in China
Age when imprisoned: 64
Marital Status: widower
Able to read: no
Able to write: no
Height: 5 foot 3 ⅝ inches
Weight: 109 ¼ lbs
Hair: Black and gray

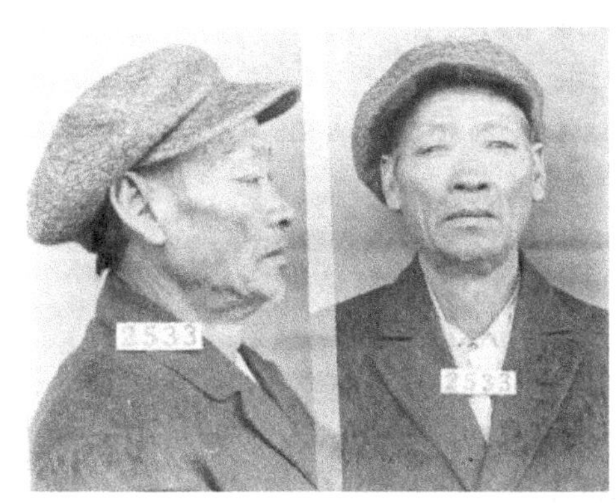

Complexion: Chinese
Eyes: brown, right eye sightless
Occupation: Laundry, kitchen helper
Died: 30 May 1915 on McNeil Island, Pierce, Washington from Cirrhosis of the Liver

29. **Name: Charles Mitchell**
Conviction: Inciting Riot in Haimes Mission, Alaska
Sentenced: 19 February 1915 for 3 years
Plead: not guilty
Discharge for good behavior: 15 June 1917
Born: 1896 Alaska
Age when imprisoned: 19
Marital Status: married
Able to read: little english
Able to write: name only
Height: 5 foot 3 ½ inches
Weight: 136 ¼ lbs
Hair: Black
Complexion: Indian
Eyes: Brown
Occupation: miner and boatman
Died: 20 September 1916 on McNeil Island, Pierce, Washington from Pulmonary Tuberculosis

30. **Name: Julio Abasca**
Conviction: Robbery in Juneau, Alaska
Sentenced: 11 January 1918 for 4 years
Plead: not guilty
Discharge for good behavior: 25 March 1921
Born: June 1891 in Chile
Age when imprisoned: 26
Marital Status: single
Able to read: no
Able to write: no
Height: 5 foot 6 ¼ inches
Weight: 161 ¼ lbs
Hair: black
Complexion: dark
Eyes: brown
Occupation: farmer and cook
Died: 5 May 1918 on McNeil Island, Pierce, Washington from Septic Pneumonia following influenza

31. **Name: Nicholas Anthony**
Conviction: Rape in Nome, Alaska
Sentenced: 6 April 1917 for 3 years
Plead: guilty
Discharged for good behavior: 28 July 1919
Born: May 1899 in St Michael, Alaska
Age when imprisoned: 20
Marital Status: single
Parents: Susan Clark
Able to read: Yes
Able to write: yes
Height: 5 foot 3 1/2 inches
Weight: 133 lbs
Hair: black
Complexion: Eskimo
Eyes: brown
Occupation: freighting, labor, and dishwasher
Died: 11 June 1918 on McNeil Island, Pierce, Washington from Pulmonary Hemorrhage

32. **Name: Ramon Gomez**
Conviction: Larceny in Juneau, Alaska
Sentenced: 10 November 1916 for 5 years
Plead: not guilty
Discharge for good behavior: 3 August 1920
Born: 4 January 1887 in Mexico
Age when imprisoned: 29
Parents: Cecencio Gomez
Marital Status: single
Able to read: no
Able to write: no
Height: 5 foot 3 ¾ inches
Weight: 136 ¼ lbs
Hair: black
Complexion: dark brown
Eyes: dark brown
Occupation: Farmer
Died: 3 May 1918 on McNeil Island, Pierce, Washington from Pneumonia Septic following Influenza

33. **Name: Daniel T Moon**
Conviction: Forgery in Fort Shafter, Hawaii Islands
Sentenced: 21 September 1918 for 4 years
Plead: guilty

Discharge for good behavior: 19 October 1921
Born: 18 April 1892 Pittsburgh. Allegheny, Pennsylvania
Age when imprisoned: 26
Marital Status: married
Able to read: yes
Able to write: yes
Height: 5 foot 9 ½ inches
Weight: 125 lbs
Hair: light brown
Complexion: light
Eyes: light blue
Occupation: Panter (keeper of the pantry): cook
and milker
Died: 11 March 1919 on McNeil Island, Pierce, Washington from Perforation of stomach and
peritonitis

David was in the Army and arrived in Hawaii in June of 1916. He worked in the hospital corps.

34. **Name: Ray Magee McKaynias**
Conviction: Stealing Interstate Freight in Huntington, Oregon
Sentenced: 4 May 1918 for 18 months
Plead: guilty
Discharge for good behavior: 19 July 1919
Born: 8 August 1884 Victoria, Lunenburg, Virginia
Age when imprisoned: 33
Marital Status: single
Able to read: yes
Able to write: yes
Height: 5 foot 9 1/16 inches
Weight: 153 ¼ lbs
Hair: brown gray at temples
Complexion: medium
Eyes: blue gray
Occupation: railroad switchman and city teamster
Died: 9 May 1919 on McNeil Island, Pierce, Washington from crushing of chest accidental
Inflicted while moving pump head at McNeil's Penitentiary

35. **Name: Angelino Callistri**
Conviction: Counterfeiting Coins Cassission in Calexico, California
Sentenced: 14 June 1919 for 4 years
Plead: not guilty
Discharge for good behavior: 21 July 1922
Born: 9 March 1879 in Italy

Age when imprisoned: 40
Marital Status: married
Wife: Alameda Dallistri Luca Magiano
Able to read: no
Able to write: no
Height: 5 foot 6 ½ inches
Weight: 179 lbs
Hair: very dark brown and gray
Complexion: dark
Eyes: brown
Occupation: miner and farmer
Died: 13 January 1920 on McNeil Island, Pierce, Washington from accidental mimes received in a fall about 30 feet abdominal hemorrhage from injury to nusentery.

36. **Name: John Cooper**
Conviction: Murder in Fairbanks, Alaska
Sentenced: 25 September 1912 for Natural life
Plead: not guilty
Discharge for good behavior: life
Born: 12 March 1871 Montreal, Quebec, Canada
Age when imprisoned: 41
Marital Status: widower
Parents: Henry Cooper
Able to read: no
Able to write: no
Height: 5 foot 6 ⅜ inches
Weight: 141
Hair: black, bald back of forehead
Complexion: black
Eyes: brown
Occupation: concrete finisher
Died: 22 February 1920 on McNeil Island, Pierce, Washington from surgical shock following an operation for carcinoma of the bowel.

37. **Name: Charles Davis**
Conviction: Violation of Harrison Narcotic Act in San Diego, California
Sentenced: 2 May 1921 for 18 months
Plead: guilty
Discharge for good behavior: 26 July 1922
Born: 2 May 1866 in Oregon City, Holt, Missouri
Age when imprisoned: 55
Marital Status: single
Able to read: no

Able to write: no
Height: 5 foot 5 inches
Weight: 85
Hair: Dark gray
Complexion: dark
Eyes: blue
Occupation:
Died: 5 Aug 1921 on McNeil Island, Pierce, Washington with Bright's Disease

38. **Name: Evert Impyn**

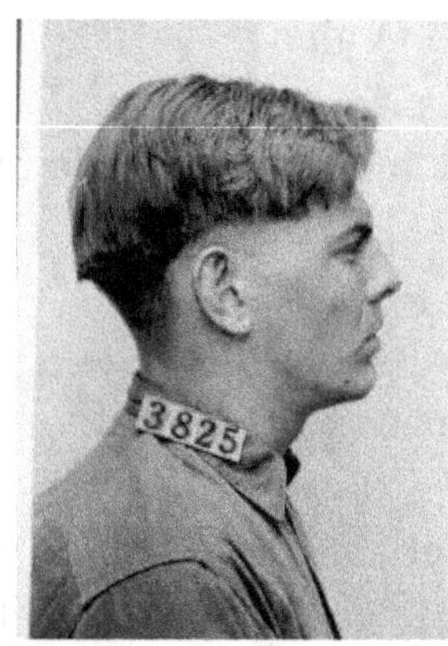

Conviction: Rape in Tacoma, Washington
Sentenced: 9 July 1921 for life
Plead: Not guilty
Discharge for good behavior: life
Born: 11 August 1899 in Harlem, Holland
Age when imprisoned: 21
Marital Status: single
Parents: Ysbrand Impyn
Able to read: yes
Able to write: yes
Height: 5 foot 11 ¼ inches
Weight: 164 ½ lbs
Hair: blonde
Complexion: light
Eyes: blue gray
Occupation: machinist helper and Marine engine oiler
Died: 5 September 1921 on McNeil Island, Pierce, Washington shot and killed while attempting to escape

When a prisoner died the other prisoners could go to the burial if they wanted. When Everett was buried two trustees and the chaplain were the only ones there. The Chaplain said a few words and then the trustees buried the body. Everett and Lawardus Hogart, his companion in crime were former soldiers who brutally attacked a man and raped the girl he was with a civilian nurse at Camp Lewis. Everett and Lawardus were both shot trying to escape from prison. Everett died from his wounds and Lawardus was sent to Leavenworth Penitentiary after he recovered from his wounds. When Everett and Lawardus joined the army they lost their Netherlands citizenship. When they were convicted of rape they lost their US citizenship. After about 17 years in Leavenworth Lawardus was exported back to the Netherlands He hoped they would grant him citizenship again. When Evert and Lawardus were arrested they were put in jail in the main cell. They were almost killed before they were moved to a smaller cell. One prisoner who was there for murder made the first attack on the two. He said, " My crime was pretty bad, but there are worse things than murder, and I would like to help give those fellows what they deserve." Another prisoner in another cell, who was serving 4 months for larceny, said, " I would be glad to take four more months just to get a crack at them birds. I been in pretty tough places, but nothing like this ever crossed my path before."

39. **Name: William Harris**
Conviction: Violation of Harrison Narcotic Act in Seattle, Washington
Sentenced: 12 Dec 1921 for 15 months
Plead: not guilty
Discharged for good behavior: 4 Dec 1922
Born: 22 August 1890 Haven, Montana
Age when imprisoned: 30
Marital Status: married
Spouse: Christina
Able to read: yes
Able to write: yes
Height: 5 foot 8 ½ inches
Weight: 140 lbs
Hair: black
Complexion: Negro
Eyes: brown
Occupation: waiter, cook, and butcher
Died: 10 May 1922 McNeil Island, Pierce, Washington from Ruptured aneurysm

40. **Name: Eubierto L Hifsas**
Conviction: Manslaughter in Juneau, Alaska
Sentenced: 10 October 1919 for 6 years
Plead: not guilty
Discharge for good behavior: 20 March 1924
Born: 16 March 1898 Philippine Islands
Age when imprisoned: 21
Marital Status: single
Parents: Jose Hifsas
Able to read: yes
Able to write: yes
Height: 5 foot 3 ½ inches
Weight: 119 ¾ lbs
Hair: black
Complexion: Philippino
Eyes: Brown
Occupation: Houter Machine
Died: 30 March 1923 on McNeil Island, Pierce, Washington from some infection precessing chronic nycardalis

41. **Name: Clarence M Ernst**

Conviction: Violation of Jones-Miller law that doubled the punishment of the Harrison narcotic enactment.
Sentenced: 2 March 1923 for 8 years
Born: 10 February 1861 Montgomery, Alabama
Marital Status: Married
Hair: black
Complexion: black
Occupation: Dining Car Porter
Died: 26 October 1923 on McNeil Island, Pierce, Washington from Exposure

Clarence was caught bringing heroin and morphine across the line at Calexico in his locker on the train where he was a porter.

42.   **Name: Luis Cardenas**
Conviction: Violated Harrison Narcotic Act in Los Angeles, California
Sentenced: 17 September 1923 for 3 years
Plead: guilty
Discharge for good behavior: 18 March 1926
Born: 19 August 1900 in Santa Ana, Mexico
Age when imprisoned: 23
Parents: Maria Cardenas
Marital Status: single
Parents: Maria Billalobos
Able to read: yes
Able to write: yes
Height: 5 foot 5 ¾ inches
Weight: 107
Hair: black
Complexion: Mexican
Eyes: dark brown
Occupation: laborer worker in cannary
Died: 5 June 1924 on McNeil Island, Pierce, Washington from Pulmonary tuberculosis

43.   **Name: Paul Dienz**
Conviction: Violated Harrison Narcotic Act in Los Angeles, California
Sentenced: 4 September 1923 for 2 years
Plead: guilty
Discharge for good behavior: 25 April 1925
Born: 29 June 1902 El Paso, Texas
Age when imprisoned: 22
Marital Status: single
Able to read: yes
Able to write: yes

Height: 5 foot 10 inches
Weight: 140
Hair: black
Complexion: mexican
Eyes: brown
Occupation: molder
Died: 19 August 1924 on McNeil Island, Pierce, Washington from Tuberculosis pulmonalis

44. **Name: Victor Guitierrez**
Conviction: Violation Harrison Narcotic Act and Opium Act in Los Angeles, California
Sentenced: 7 September 1923 for 3 years
Plead: guilty
Discharge for good behavior: 7 January 1926
Born: 30 August 1900 Guatemala, Central America
Age when imprisoned: 23
Marital Status: single
Able to read: no
Able to write: no
Height: 5 foot 7 ½ inches
Weight: 151
Hair: black
Complexion: mexican
Eyes: dark brown
Occupation: blacksmith
Died: 26 December 1924 on McNeil Island, Pierce, Washington from Pulmonary tuberculosis.

45. **Name: Anton Dolchok**
Conviction: Murder 2nd Degree in Seldovia, Alaska
Sentenced: 15 December 1922 for natural life
Plead: guilty
Discharge for good behavior: natural life
Born: 5 July 1896 Seldovia, Kenai Peninsula Borough, Alaska
Age when imprisoned: 26
Marital Status: single
Able to read: yes
Able to write: yes
Height: 5 foot 4 inches
Weight: 124 lbs
Hair: black
Complexion: indian
Eyes: dark brown
Occupation: marine fireman and miner
Died: 5 May 1925 on McNeil Island, Pierce, Washington from tuberculosis.

46.   **Name: O Itow**
Conviction: Murder 1st degree in Juneau, Alaska
Sentenced: 11 Feb 1913 to be hung then changed to life
Plead: not guilty
Discharge for good behavior: life
Age when imprisoned: 30
Born: 22 Feb 1886 Japan
Marital Status: single\
Parents: R Itow
Able to read: yes
Able to write: yes
Height: 5 foot 2 ¾ inches
Weight: 111
Hair: black
Complexion: Japanese
Eyes: brown
Teeth: good condition, none missing
Occupation: cannery man
Died: 18 Dec 1926 on McNeil Island, Pierce, Washington from Tuberculosis

O was sentenced to be hung for the murder in 1912. The judge set the date of March 1913, but the exchange says they have to wait 3 years so the date is now on Feb. 18th 1916. Again his date was changed to 17th of April 1916, but on the 14th of April he was handed a telegram changing his sentence from hanging to life in prison from President Wilson upon the request of the Japanese Ambassador.

47.   **Name: Joe Loco**
Conviction: Rape in Seldovia, Alaska
Sentenced: 25 October 1926 for 10 years
Plead: not guilty
Discharge for good behavior: 12 July 1933
Born: 9 January 1902 Seldovia, Alaska
Age when imprisoned:25
Marital Status: single
Able to read: yes
Able to write: yes
Height: 5 foot 4 inches
Weight: 137 ½ lbs
Hair: black
Complexion: indian
Eyes: brown
Occupation: shoe maker

Died: 1 March 1928 on McNeil Island, Pierce, Washington from Tublerculosis with acute pulmonary hemorrhage

48. **Name: J L Beckham**
Conviction: Violation Drug Acts in Bisbee, Arizona
Sentenced: 23 May 1927 for 2 years
Plead:guilty
Discharge for good behavior: 23 December 1928
Born: 26 February 1872 in Summit Point, Jefferson, West Virginia
Age when imprisoned: 56
Marital Status: widower
Able to read: yes
Able to write: yes
Height: 5 foot 9 inches
Weight: 127 lbs
Hair: gray
Complexion: sallow
Eyes: gray
Occupation: carpenter
Died: 4 April 1928 on McNeil Island, Pierce, Washington from Bright's Disease (prison records) Chromia Pulmonary Tuberculosis Empyema left side Chronic Nephritis Morphias (death certificate)

49. **Name: Robert Franklin Davidson**
Conviction: Violation Drug Act in Seattle Washington
Sentence: 9 March 1928 for 1 year and 1 day
Plead: guilty
Discharged for good behavior: 27 Dec 1928
Born: August 1896 Kaliespell, Flathead, Montana
Age when imprisoned: 31
Marital Status: Married
Parents: Alfred Davidson and Flora Loesa Stahl
Able to read: yes
Able to write: yes
Height: 5 Foot 4 ¾ inches
Weight: 156 lbs
Hair: Dark
Complexion:Ruddy
Eyes: Gray
Occupation: mechanic
Died: 13 May 1928 McNeil Island, Pierce, Washington from Hemorrhage Right Pleura from Carcinoma of Pancreas Cosinora Mediastinum Empyema Right Pleura

50. **Name: Timothy Dienouluck**
Conviction: Murder Second Degree in Lower Yukon River, Alaska
Sentenced: 12 September 1925 for 15 years
Plead: guilty
Discharge for good behavior: 8 October 1935
Born: 1901 Alaska
Age when imprisoned: 24
Marital Status: married
Able to read: no
Able to write: no
Height: 5 foot 7 ¼ inches
Weight: 151 lbs
Hair: black
Complexion: eskimo
Eyes: brown
Occupation: hunter
Died: 19 August 1928 on McNeil Island, Pierce, Washington from Generalized miliary tuberculosis of both lungs, liver, spleen, kidneys, and visceral and parietal peritoneum

Timothy was arrested for shooting the tribe medicine man. Timothy claimed his father died from a spell cast upon him by the magician. He hoped to learn a trade in prison.

51. **Name: William Johnson,**
Alias: "Snoose" Johnson and Robert O'Brien. Birth Name: Robert Lindquist
Conviction: Violation Postal Laws in Portland, Oregon
Sentenced: 3 July 1928 for 7 years
Plead: guilty
Discharge for good behavior: 2 September 1933
Born: 22 August 1895 Duluth,St Louis, Minnesota
Age when imprisoned: 32
Marital Status: single
Parents: Lindquist
Able to read: yes
Able to write: yes
Height: 5 foot 4 ¼ inches
Weight: 122
Hair: brown
Complexion: sallow
Eyes: blue
Occupation: waiter
Died: 21 August 1928 on McNeil Island, Pierce, Washington from acute endocarditis contributory of Streptococcic septicemic from gunshot wound in left elbow

William was involved in a gunfight with police outside his hotel on 29 May 1928. He was the leader of a gang who robbed Portland, Oregon post offices. William shot one of the detectives in the leg. William had been shot in the neck, lungs, and arm. It was believed he would not live. On the 30 of May it was reported that Williams would survive his wounds.

52. **Name: James Kelly**
Alias: Dan Fullinan
Conviction: Violation Drug Act in San Francisco, California
Sentenced: 28 December 1926 for 5 years
Plead: guilty
Discharge for good behavior: 3 October 1930
Born: 15 August 1884 New York, New York
Age when imprisoned:42
Marital Status: single
Able to read: yes
Able to write: yes
Height: 5 foot 4 inches
Weight: 125 ½ lbs
Hair: dark brown
Complexion: fair
Eyes: hazel
Occupation: teamster
Died: 14 July 1929 on McNeil Island, Pierce, Washington from Laryngeal Tuberculosis contributory endo-Carditis, drug addiction

53. **Name: Levi R Adams**
Conviction: Violation National Motor Vehicle Theft Act in Vernonia, Oregon
Sentenced: 10 May 1929 for 2 years
Plead: guilty
Discharge for good behavior: 17 December 1930
Born: 2 April 1896 Chicago, Cook, Illinois
Age when imprisoned: 33
Marital Status: married
Wife: Louise Harriett Taylor
Able to read: yes
Able to write: yes
Height: 5 foot 7 inches
Weight: 161 lbs
Hair: black
Complexion: dark
Eyes: brown
Occupation: truck driver and barber
Died: 1 August 1929 on McNeil Island, Pierce, Washington from Pulmonary Tuberculosis

54. **Name: Gabriel Espinosa**
Conviction: Violation Revenue Laws in Naco, Arizona
Sentenced: 18 February 1929 for 16 months
Plead: guilty
Discharge for good behavior: 18 March 1930
Born: 18 March 1893 Batuso, Sonora, Mexico
Age when imprisoned: 35
Marital Status: married
Wife: Josefa
Able to read: 2 years of grade school in Mexico
Able to write: 2 years of grade school in Mexico
Height: 5 foot 4 inches
Weight: 110
Hair: black
Complexion: Mexico
Eyes: brown
Occupation: Miner
Died: 7 October 1929 on McNeil Island, Pierce, Washington from Chronic Pulmonary Tuberculosis contributory Gastric Ulcers of Stomach

55. **Name: Lewis Jackson Echols**
Conviction: Violation National Prohibition Act in Wallace, Idaho
Sentenced: 1 June 1929 for 15 months and fined $1200
Plead: not guilty
Discharge for good behavior: 10 July 1930
Born: 12 August 1873 Rome,
Age when imprisoned: 55
Marital Status: separated
Parents: Louis Barton Echols and Emily Jane Weems
Wife: Catherine Marie Dunne
School: 7th grade
Able to read: yes
Able to write: yes
Height: 5 foot 11 inches
Weight: 164 lbs
Hair: Iron gray
Complexion: shallow
Eyes: blue gray
Occupation: miner
Died: 12 June 1930 on McNeil Island, Pierce, Washington from Pulmonary tuberculosis

Lewis, better known as Jack, was a miner and supplemented his income making and distributing alcohol. His wife was the widow of his brother Albert. She and Albert had two children. After they married Jack and Catherine had two more of their own.

56. **Name: Frank Kuhn**
True Name: Frank Kuhen
Conviction: Violation National Prohibition Act in Flagstaff, Arizona
Sentenced: 26 July 1929 for 15 months
Plead: guilty
Discharge for good behavior: 9 September 1930
Born: 30 April 1886 Fort Worth, Tarrant, Texas
Age when imprisoned: 43
Marital Status: single
School: 5th grade
Able to read: yes
Able to write: yes
Height: 5 foot 9 ¼ inches
Weight: 147 lbs
Complexion: ruddy
Eyes: brown
Occupation: laborer
Died: 23 August 1930 on McNeil Island, Pierce, Washington from CerebroSpinal Syphilis contributory Bronchopneumonia

57. **Name: Walter Thompson,**
Alias: R King
Conviction: Violation Immigration in San Diego, California
Sentenced: 21 January 1930 for 4 years
Discharge for good behavior: 30 March 1933
Born: 20 February 1896 Wellston, Jackson, Ohio
Age when imprisoned: 33
Marital Status: single
School: 6th grade
Able to read: yes
Able to write: yes
Height: 5 foot 4 ¼ inches
Weight: 136
Hair: dark chestnut
andComplexion: medium yellow
Eyes: dark chestnut
Occupation: waiter
Died: 8 September 1930 on McNeil Island, Pierce, Washington from Angina Pectoris contributory Acute Gastritis

58. **Name: Roy Brennan**
   Birth Name: Roy Brennan Thomas
   Conviction: Violation Drug Act in San Francisco, California
   Sentenced: 21 Dec 1929 for 3 years
   Discharged for good behavior: 12 April 1932
   Born: 31 July 1877 Junction City, Geary, Kansas
   Age when imprisoned: 53
   Parents: M C Thomas
   Marital Status: married
   Spouse: M
   School: 8th grade
   Able to read: yes
   Able to write:yes
   Height: 5 foot 9 ½ inches
   Weight: 156 lbs
   Complexion:florid
   Eyes: Pale blue
   Occupation: Laborer
   Died: 3 Nov 1930 on McNeil Island, Pierce, Washington from Cerebral Hemorrhage contributory General Arterio-aclerosis

59. **Name: Harry Levos**
   Alias: Harry the Greek
   Conviction: Violation Drug Act in San Francisco, California
   Sentenced: 10 January 1929 for 3 years
   Plead: guilty
   Discharge for good behavior: 11 May 1931
   Born: 25 August 1883 Zande Island, Greece
   Age when imprisoned: 25
   School:7th grade in Greece
   Able to read: yes
   Able to write: yes
   Height: 5 foot 8 ¾ inches
   Weight: 142
   Hair: black
   Complexion: slightly dark
   Eyes: brown
   Occupation: Barber
   Died: 10 January 1931 on McNeil Island, Pierce, Washington from Broncho-pneumonia

Harry was arrested after selling a good amount of drugs to a Federal agent. Harry was known as a thief and had already been in jail for drug dealing and pleaded for leniency because of illness. The plea was flatly denied.

60. **Name: Edwin Abert**
Conviction: Larceny in Nome, Alaska
Sentenced: 24 September 1930 for 3 years 6 months
Discharge for good behavior: 2 June 1930
Born: September 1910 Nome, Alaska
Age when imprisoned: 20
Marital Status: single
Able to read: no
Able to write: no
Occupation: miner
Died: 26 March 1931 on McNeil Island, Pierce, Washington from Pulmonary Tuberculosis

61. **Name: Frank W Brown**
Conviction: Violation Drug Act in Dunsmuir, California
Sentenced: 21 August 1929 for 3 years
Plead: guilty
Discharge for good behavior: 14 January 1932
Born: 10 March 1898 Chicago, Cook, Illinois
Age when imprisoned: 32
Marital Status: single
School: 10th grade
Able to read: yes
Able to write: yes
Height: 5 foot 6 ¾ inches
Weight: 161 lbs
Hair: black
Complexion: light
Eyes: blue
Occupation: laborer
Died: 29 April 1931 on McNeil Island, Pierce, Washington from Chronic Endo-carditic Contributory Syphilis

62. **Name: Frank Kelly**
Conviction: Violation Drug Act in San Francisco, California
Sentenced: 15 February 1930 for 5 years
Discharge for good behavior: 5 November 1933
Born: 23 July 1884 in Boston, Sussex, Massachusetts
Age when imprisoned: 45
Marital Status: single

School: 8th grade
Able to read: yes
Able to write: yes
Height: 5 foot 8 ¼ inches
Weight: 145 lbs
Complexion: shallow
Eyes: hazel gray
Occupation: Hospital orderly
Died: 24 July 1931 on McNeil Island, Pierce, Washington from Chronic Myocarditis

63. **Name: Earl A Elliott**
Conviction: National Probation Act in Walla Walla, Washington
Sentenced: May 1931 for 15 months
Discharge for good behavior: 15 July 1932
Born: 11 August 1902 in Pomeroy, Garfield, Washington
Age when imprisoned: 27
Marital Status: single
Parents: Robert Ernest Elliot and Roberta Pearl Ruth Hill
Able to read: yes
Able to write: yes
Height: 5 foot 8 ¼ inches
Weight: 152 lbs
Hair: black
Complexion:
Eyes: dark gray
Occupation: Ranch Hand
Died: 11 August 1931 on McNeil Island, Pierce, Washington from accidental drowning

64. **Name**: **Ben Carrothers**
Conviction: National Prohibition Act in Pocatello, Idaho
Sentenced: 14 March 1931 for 18 months
Discharge for good behavior: 10 July 1932
Born: 24 November 1879 in Texas
Age when imprisoned: 31
Marital Status: married
Wife: Nancy and Lola B
School: 8th grade
Able to read: yes
Able to write: yes
Height: 5 foot 7 ¾ inches
Weight: 185
Hair: black
Complexion: black

Eyes: black
Occupation: Cook
Died: 30 April 1932 on McNeil Island, Pierce, Washington from Valvulas heart disease combined lesions aortic and mitral Myocarditis chronic Nephritis, interstitial, chronic Asthma, Cardiac contributory Embolism - cerebral

Ben's trial was the last one for the Judge. Ben was a repeat violator and the trial took one afternoon.

65.   **Name: Thomas F Harrington**
Conviction: Embezzlement in Schofield Barracks, Hawaii
Sentenced: 8 April 1928 for 10 years
Plead: not guilty
Discharge for good behavior: 24 December 1933
Born: 21 September 1891 Paterson, Passaic, New Jersey
Age when imprisoned: 36
Marital Status: single
Able to read: yes
Able to write: yes
Height: 5 foot 11 inches
Weight: 135 ½ lbs
Hair: black
Complexion: ruddy
Eyes: brown
Occupation: bookkeeper
Died: 29 September 1932 on McNeil Island, Pierce, Washington from Enteroposis, Duodenal ulcer, acute general Peritonitis contritonitis Operation for fixation of colon Ileus

Thomas was earlier convicted of embezzling Army property while in service . He asked that he not be paroled on a precious sentence , because he was scared of the husband of a woman he had an affair with.

66.   **Name: John Riley**
Conviction: National Motor Vehicle Theft Act in Tucson, Arizona
Sentenced: 22 June 1932 for 1 year and 1 day
Discharge for good behavior: 8 May 1933
Born: 4 October 1898 Lawrence Co., Ohio
Age when imprisoned: 33
Marital Status: single
Parents: I J Riley and Mary Mille
Able to read: yes
Able to write: yes
Height: 6 foot 1 inch

Weight: 196 lbs
Hair: dark
Complexion: medium dark
Eyes: dark gray
Occupation: farmer
Died: 12 January 1933 on McNeil Island, Pierce, Washington from Acute Yellow Atrophy of Liver, Syphilis

67. **Name**: **Henry Williams**
Born: 29 November 1880 Gold Hill, Storey, Nevada
Occupation: Cook
Died: 28 January 1933 on McNeil Island, Pierce, Washington from Chronic Myocarditis, Chronic Nephritis contributory Ascites

68. **Name: Feliciano Constantino**
Conviction: Counterfeiting in San Francisco, California
Sentenced: 30 July 1932 for 3 years 6 months
Discharge for good behavior: 10 May 1935
Born: October 1908 in Philippine Islands
Age when imprisoned: 22
Marital Status: single
Able to read: yes
Able to write: yes
Height: 5 foot 4 inches
Weight: 145
Hair: black
Complexion: dark brown
Occupation: Showcard writer, Commercial Artist
Died: 9 July 1933 on McNeil Island, Pierce, Washington from Asthma, Bronchial contributory Myocarditis, Dementia Praecox

69. **Name: Albert Grant**
Conviction: 2nd degree murder in Sitka, Alaska
Sentenced: 13 November 1928 for 15 years
Plead: not guilty
Discharge for good behavior: 13 December 1938
Born: 1875 Chichagof Island, Alaska
Age when imprisoned: 53
Marital Status: widower
Wife: Uerin
School: 1st grade
Able to read: yes
Able to write: yes

Height: 5 foot 7 ¼ inches
Weight: 177
Hair: black
Complexion: Swarthy
Eyes: brown
Occupation: barber and deck hand
Died: 27 February 1934 on McNeil Island, Pierce, Washington from Carcinoma of Stomach, chronic Myocarditis

70. **Name: Edward Cook**
Conviction: Counterfeiting in Martinez, California
Sentenced: 16 June 1933 for 5 years
Discharge for good behavior: 23 March 1937
Born: 1882 Ardmore, Carter, Oklahoma
Age when imprisoned: 52
Marital Status:
Parents: Clay Cook and Corrine Fishbone
Height: 5 foot 10 ¼ inches
Weight: 190
Hair: Dark Chestnut gray edges
Complexion: dark
Eyes: dark brown
Died: 19 April 1934 on McNeil Island, Pierce, Washington from Ulcer of the Stomach with perforation,acute general Peritonitis, Operation Gastroenterostomy, gastrorrhaphy

71. **Name: John Alexander**
Conviction: Manslaughter in Fairbanks, Alaska
Sentenced: 31 January 1931 for 9 years
Discharge for good behavior: 18 September 1938
Born: 1903 in Fort Noken, Alaska
Age when imprisoned: 28
Marital Status: Married
Wife: Laura Jonas
Able to read: no
Able to write: no
Height: 5 foot 5 ½ inches
Weight: 145
Hair: black
Complexion: light brown
Eyes: dark brown
Occupation: carpenter
Died: 5 May 1934 on McNeil Island, Pierce, Washington from Tuberculosis of the Lungs and of the bones

John was arrested for hitting his nephew over the head with a piece of wood in a drunken brawl killing him.

72. **Name: Charles Harry Hodge**
Conviction: Impersonating Federal Officer in Bridgeport, Washington
Sentenced: 28 August 1931 for 6 years
Discharge for good behavior: 7 February 1836
Born: 13 December 1865 in Packwaukee,Wisconsin
Age when imprisoned: 66
Marital Status: widower
Parents: S M and Adie
Able to read: yes
Able to write: yes
Height: 5 foot 7 ½ inches
Weight: 208 ½ lbs
Hair: Gray
Complexion: florid
Eyes: Hazel gray
Occupation: cook
Died: 15 June 1934 on McNeil Island, Pierce, Washington from 3rd Cerebral Hemorrhage and Arteriosclerosis-Cerebral

Charles had been committing crimes since 1897. His list of crimes took over 5 minutes to read in court. This time he acted as a secret service agent. He was serving two consecutive three years sentences.

73. **Name: Roy Cook**
Conviction: White Slave Act in Portland Oregon
Sentenced: 12 October 1934 for 22 months
Discharge for good behavior: 1 April 1936
Born: 15 March 1885 Keytesville, Missouri
Age when imprisoned: 49
Marital Status: single
Parents: Morris and Mary
Able to read: yes
Able to write: yes
Height: 5 foot 10 inches
Weight: 191
Hair: black
Complexion: dark brown
Eyes: dark
Occupation: cook

Died: 12 March 1935 on McNeil Island, Pierce, Washington from Chronic Myocarditis with decompensation

74. **Name: Henry Clinton**
Born: 1908
Died: 28 October 1935 on McNeil Island, Pierce, Washington from Chronic Appendicitis Operation Peritonitis

75. **Name: Thomas Jones**
Born: 1866 in Missouri
Marital Status: single
Able to read: yes
Able to write: yes
Height: 5 foot 4 ½ inches
Weight: 116 lbs
Hair: very light brown
Complexion: fair
Eyes: blue
Occupation: umbrella maker
Died: 2 March 1936 on McNeil Island, Pierce, Washington from Chronic hypertrophy of prostate

76. **Name: John Peter Freihage**
Conviction: Manslaughter in Ruby, Alaska then Fairbanks, Alaska
Sentenced: 21 Feb 1931 for 10 years then changed 30 Jan 1933 for 20 years
Discharged for good behavior: 7 Oct 1939
Born: 29 February 1876 Beloit, Mitchell, Kansas
Age when imprisoned: 56
Marital Status: Married
Parents: John Conrad Freihage and Maria Gesina Cronin
Wife: May
Education: 6 grade
Height: 5' 7'
Weight: 187
Hair: Dark and Gray
Complexion: Dark
Eyes: Gray
Died: 23 February 1937 on McNeil Island, Pierce, Washington from Carcinoma of lung, Metastasis on cervical vertebrae

77. **Name: William Henry Johnstone**
Conviction: Forgery in Salt Lake City,Utah
Sentenced: 27 April 1935 for 5 years and $100 fine
Discharge for good behavior: 2 February 1939

Born: 29 December 1904 in Salt Lake City, Salt Lake, Utah
Able to read: yes
Able to write: yes
Height: 5 foot 6 ¼ inches
Weight: 141
Hair: dark c
Complexion: m dark
Eyes: light brown
Occupation: nurse
Died: 29 April 1937 on McNeil Island, Pierce, Washington from accidental Traumatism by crushing from a landslide

William forged a name on a $25 C C C pay check. After his death the US senate and representatives passed a bill giving William's son 3500 dollars. William died in a landslide while digging a trench In prison. It looks like William was born William Henry Denhalter son of Charles Henry Denhalter and Julia Rosa, daughter of the cleaning lady. When the baby was three days old he was given to Mr and Mrs John Henry Johnstone.

78.   **Name: Moses Phillips**
Conviction: Manslaughter in Hoonah Alaska
Sentenced: 15 December 1934 for 5 years
Discharge for good behavior: 21 August 1938
Born: 25 January 1913 in Alaska
Age when imprisoned: 21
Parents: Henry John K Phillips and Mary
Marital Status: Single
Able to read: yes
Able to write: yes
Height: 5 foot 6 ¾ inches
Weight: 165 lbs
Hair: black
Complexion: dark
Occupation: fisherman
Died: 30 May 1937 on McNeil Island, Pierce, Washington from strangulation by suicidal hanging

79.   **Name: Jonathan Kayogok**
Conviction: Murder 2nd degree in Nunivak Island, Alaska
Sentenced: 19 October 1932 for 30 years
Discharge for good behavior: 9 December 1952
Born: 1910 Nunivak Island, Alaska
Age when imprisoned: 22
Marital Status: single

Able to read: no
Able to write: no
Height: 6 foot 1 ¼ inches
Weight: 141 lbs
Hair: black
Complexion: light yellow
Eyes: dark brown
Occupation: fisherman
Died: 3 July 1937 on McNeil Island, Pierce, Washington from Pulmonary Tuberculosis, Bilateral

80. **Name: Lawrence Russell Royal**
Conviction: White Slave Act in Arlingtion, Oregon
Sentenced: 3 July 1936 for 3 years 6 months
Discharge for good behavior: 14 March 1939
Born: 9 August 1909 in United States
Age when imprisoned: 26
Marital Status: divorced
Parents: Leader George Royal and Mabel Bertine Olsen
Wife: Helen Louise Core
Able to read: yes
Able to write: yes
Height: 5 foot 5 ½ inches
Weight: 151
Hair: dark Blond
Complexion: fair
Eyes: hazel
Occupation: truck driver
Died: 14 March 1938 on McNeil Island, Pierce, Washington from Chronic Parenchymatous Nephritis

81. **Name: Fred Amos**
Conviction: selling liquor to Indiana in Burns, Oregon
Sentenced: 18 December 1937 for 1 year and 1 day
Discharge for good behavior: 7 November 1938
Born: 29 September 1892 in Cape Charles, Northampton, Virginia
Age when imprisoned: 46
Marital Status: single
Able to read: yes
Able to write: yes
Height: 5 foot 10 ½ inches
Weight: 135 lbs
Hair: chestnut
Complexion: brown

Eyes: chestnut
Occupation: Railroader
Died: 29 April 1938 on McNeil Island, Pierce, Washington from Coronary Thombonio

82. **Name: Steve LaFave**
Conviction: Official records claimed he was a transient. He was from Portland, Oregon to Prison Camp at Fort Lewis
Length in time in USP: 1 month
Born: 12 December 1888 in Michigan
Occupation: Laborer and cook
Died: 22 May 1938 on Federal Prison Camp, DuPont, Pierce, Washington
Buried: McNeil Island, Pierce, Washington

83. **Name: George A Dinsmore**
Conviction: Rape in Tanana, Alaska
Sentenced: 2 February 1937 for 3 years
Discharge for good behavior: 25 May 1938
Born: 11 November 1860 Auburn, Androscoggin, Maine
Parents: Charles Dinsmore and Melvina M Currier
Wife: Ella J Moore
Height: 5 foot 7 ¾ inches
Weight: 193 lbs
Hair: gray bald
Complexion: medium dark
Eyes: gray
Occupation: Carpenter and barber
Died: 26 June 1938 on McNeil Island, Pierce, Washington from Cardiac disease, cardiorenal vascular

84. **Name: George H Wood**
Length in time in USP: 7 days
Born: 4 July 1895 Lennox, Lincoln, South Dakota
Marital Status: divorced
Parents: Frank Wood and Mary A Liston
Hair: Brown
Eyes: Hazel
Occupation: concrete worker and Laborer
Died: 6 July 1938 on McNeil Island, Pierce, Washington from Post-operative shock and hemorrhage. Operation was Hernioplasty for a Inguinal hernia

85. **Name: Bernard Thompson**
Conviction: Postal breaking and entering in Defiance, Arizona
Sentenced: 22 January 1938 for 1 year and 1 day

Discharge for good behavior: 11 November 1938
Born: 10 February 1907 in United States
Age when imprisoned: 31
Marital Status:single
Parents: Na-Tan-Ne Mey-De-Chi and Be-Gee-Bia
Height: 4 foot 9 inches
Weight: 130
Hair: Black
Complexion: dark
Eyes: brown
Occupation: Laborer
Died: 27 August 1938 on McNeil Island, Pierce, Washington from Pulmonary Tuberculosis

86. **Name: Harry Dickerson Red Horse**
Conviction: Larceny - Theft of Government Property
Arrested/Tried: Kern, Kansas / Prescott, Arizona
Sentenced: 11 July 1938 for 2 years
Discharge for good behavior: 17 February 1940
Born: May 1919
Age when imprisoned:
Marital Status: single
Parents: Joe Red Horse and Zam
Height: 5 foot 5 ½ inches
Weight: 117 lbs
Hair: Black
Complexion: dark yellow
Eyes: brown
Occupation: laborer
Died: 3 October 1938 on McNeil Island, Pierce, Washington from Peritonitis, local acute abscess, pelvic; cause: appendicitis, gangrenous. Acute Appendicitis had an appendectomy operation, and also had bilateral Trachoma

87. **Name: Telesfaro Badillo**
Conviction: Drug Act
Arrested/Tried: Nogalis, Arizona/Tucson, Arizona
Sentenced: 5 October 1937 for 2 years
Discharge for good behavior: 13 June 1939
Born: 5 January 1874 in Stockton, San Joaquin, Califorma
Age when imprisoned: 63
Marital Status: married
Parents: Peter Badtllo and Inocenta Luna
Wife: Aquilia Chaires
Able to read: yes

Able to write: yes
Height: 5 foot 6 ¾ inches
Weight: 140
Hair: gray
Complexion: dark yellow
Eyes: dark brown
Occupation: miner
Died: 21 March 1939 on McNeil Island, Pierce, Washington from Cerebral hemorrhage contributory chromis myocarditic, general Arteriosclerosis

88. **Name: Paul Francis White**
Conviction: Counterfeiting
Arrested/Tried: Ruch, Oregon/Portland, Oregon
Sentenced: 22 July 1933 for 10 years
Discharge for good behavior: 7 April 1940
Born: 16 September 1868 in Mount Vernon, Fairfax, Virginia
Age when imprisoned: 65
Marital Status: single
Parents: Michael White and Mary Stafford
Able to read: yes
Able to write: yes
Height: 5 foot 9 ¾ inches
Weight: 190 lbs
Hair: chestnut, white and gray top
Complexion: florid
Eyes: light brown
Occupation: Chemist
Died: 8 April 1939 on McNeil Island, Pierce, Washington from Cardiac disease, coronary occlusion, contributory general Arteriosclerosis, cardiac disease, coronary sclerosis

89. **Name: George Pope**
Conviction: Voluntary Manslaughter
Arrested/Tried: White River, Arizona/Globe, Arizona
Sentenced: 20 February 1935 for 10 years
Discharge for good behavior: 7 November 1941
Born: 15 September 1874 Arizona
Age when imprisoned: 61
Marital Status: widower
Parents: Klink-Gee-Chon and Cha-Hone-Day
Wife:Nah lene tis; Cora; Anna Gloshay
Able to read: yes
Able to write: yes
Height: 5 foot 8 ¼ inches

Weight: 190
Hair: Black
Complexion: dark yellow
Eyes: left blue and right dark brown
Occupation: blacksmith
Died: 23 May 1939 on McNeil Island, Pierce, Washington from lobulan Pneumonia, contributory Influenza, general Arteriosclerosis, and Senility

90. **Name: Ray Henry Sutley**
Conviction: Counterfeiting
Arrested/Tried: Seattle, Washington/same
Sentenced: 19 September 1938 for 15 months
Discharge for good behavior: 20 October 1939
Born: 25 March 1884 in Prospect, Marion, Ohio
Age when imprisoned: 54
Marital Status: married
Parents: John W Sutley and Eliza Matilda Henry
Wife: Florence Ople Cooperider
Height: 5 foot 7 ¼ inches
Weight: 119
Hair: gray
Complexion: medium dark
Eyes: gray
Occupation: laborer
Died: 20 July 1939 on McNeil Island, Pierce, Washington from Coronary occlusion, Hypertensive cardio-vascular disease contributory Latent syphilis, arrested pulmonary tuberculosis

91. **Name**: **Herbert Ellsworth Calvin Brock**
Length in time in USP: 2 months 3 days
Born: 25 December 1903
Military: yes Marine Corps 2 years
Marital Status: Married
Parents: Herbert R Brock and Flora Whitehill
Wife: G Nanetta Adams
Died: 31 January 1940 on McNeil Island, Pierce, Washington from Bacteremia contributory generalized subacute Arthritis

92. **Name: John Mallon Kelley**
Conviction: National Motor Vehicle Theft Act
Arrested/Tried: Salt Lake, Utah/ same
Sentenced: 27 November 1937 for 4 years
Discharge for good behavior: 25 December 1940

Born: 2 June 1901 Buffalo, Erie, New York
Age when imprisoned: 36
Marital Status: single
Parents: Grace Devere
Able to read: yes
Able to write: yes
Height: 5 foot 7 ½ inches
Weight: 156 lbs
Hair: dark brown
Complexion: fair
Eyes: dark brown
Occupation: musician
Died: 12 February 1940 on McNeil Island, Pierce, Washington from Subacute bacterial endocarditis, Cerebral embolism contributory Mitral and cardiac stenosis

93. **Name: Gustave Schultes**
Conviction: Counterfeiting
Arrested/Tried: San Francisco, California/same
Sentenced: 9 February 1934 for 10 years
Discharge for good behavior: 26 October 1940
Born: 26 March 1873 in Hanover, Germany
Age when imprisoned: 60
Marital Status: married
Parents: Otto Schultes and Marie
Wife: Fannie D
Able to read: yes
Able to write: yes
Height: 5 foot 6 inches
Weight: 189 lbs
Hair: chestnut
Complexion: shallow
Eyes: dark gray
Occupation: Druggist and Hotel Proprietor
Died: 18 September 1940 on McNeil Island, Pierce, Washington from Cardiac decompensation with edema, Coronary Disease, Auricular fibrillation, and Chronic myocarditis

At Gustave's trial, when his counterfeit partner Phyllis Rossi was on the stand, his wife stood up and accused Phyllis of breaking up her home. Phyllis pleaded guilty and turned state's evidence against Gustave.

94. **Name: Donald Raymond Leeson**
Conviction: 3 counts of Stealing mail
Length in time in USP: 25 months

Born: 28 November 1893 in Pasadena, California
Parents: Charles O Leeson and Flora B Douglas
Height: Short
Weight: Slender
Hair: Dark Brown
Eyes: Light Brown
Occupation: Salesman and Stock clerk
Died: 30 October 1940 on McNeil Island, Pierce, Washington from Concussion of the brain - possible skull fracture, colles fracture of left arm, due to a fall

95. **Name: Jesse Watson**
Conviction: Stealing construction material from a government warehouse
Born: 2 October 1886 United States
Marital Status: Married
Wife: Ruth
Occupation: lumberman
Died: 19 December 1940 on McNeil Island, Pierce, Washington from Bronchopneumonia

96. **Name: Martin Lupe**
Conviction: Murder
Arrested/Tried: Cibecue, Arizona/Globe, Arizona
Sentenced: 13 February 1936 for life
Discharge for good behavior: Life
Born: 3 October 1908 in United States
Age when imprisoned: 27
Marital Status: widow
Parents: William Lupe
Wife: Lizzie
Able to read: yes
Able to write: yes
Height: 5 foot 6 ¾ inches
Weight: 142
Hair: black
Complexion: dark yellow
Eyes: dark brown
Occupation: farmer
Died: 29 March 1941 on McNeil Island, Pierce, Washington from Miliary Tuberculosis

Martin is the son of the Apache chief. He killed his wife with an ax while in a jealous rage. Martin pleaded not guilty.

97. **Name: Bill Kanyak**
Conviction: Rape

Sentenced: for 15 years
Length in time in USP: 11 months 26 days
Born: 3 September 1913 in Solomon, Alaska
Parents: Frank Kanyak
Occupation: miner and longshoreman
Died: 6 May 1941 on McNeil Island, Pierce, Washington from Pulmonary Tuberculosis

98. **Name: Cecil Calvin Rolfe**
Conviction: Impersonating Federal Officer
Arrested/Tried: Witchuta, Kansas/Los Angeles, California
Sentenced: 4 September 1934 for 7 years 6 months
Discharge for good behavior: 13 March 1940
Born: 22 February 1882 in England
Age when imprisoned: 52
Marital Status: single
Able to read: yes
Able to write: yes
Height: 6 foot 10 inches
Weight: 176 ½ lbs
Hair: Dark brown and gray
Complexion: medium fair
Eyes: gray
Occupation: office clerk and Lawyer
Died: 10 May 1941 on McNeil Island, Pierce, Washington from Cerebral Hemorrhage

99. **Name: Bert Ellen Stockstill**
Conviction: Sodomy
Arrested/Tried: Alcatraz Island, California/San Francisco, California
Plead: not guilty
Sentence: 5 years
Born: 8 September 1882 in Carlton, Kentucky
Military: Army 7 years 6 months Private
Marital Status: single
Parents: Joseph P Stockstill and Katherine Spellman
Age when imprisoned: 41 years old
Able to read: yes
Able to write: yes
Height: 5 foot 11 inches
Weight: 167 ½ lbs
Hair: Dark brown
Complexion: inclived and ruddy
Eyes: Brown

Occupation: farmer
Died: 2 September 1942 on McNeil Island, Pierce, Washington from Carcinoma, Duodenal

100. **Name: Paul Burrwell Roubay**
Alias: Paul Burrwell Rabe Sr
Length in time in USP: 1 year 5 month 22 days
Born: 25 February 1881 New York, New York
Marital Status: married
Parents: Jonathan W L Roubay and Melvina Cassandra Lytle
Wife: Anne B Tripp
Occupation: oil promotor
Died: 5 July 1943 on McNeil Island, Pierce, Washington from Coronary Thrombosis

101. **Name: William James Young**
Length in time in USP: 22 months 12 days
Born: 1 July 1901 in Pittsburgh, Allegheny, Pennsylvania
Military: yes Army 18 years Sergeant
Occupation: U S Army service
Died: 24 September 1943 on McNeil Island, Pierce, Washington from subacute bacterial endocarditis due to Old Mitral heart disease

102. **Name: Robert C Miller**
Length in time in USP: 5 months 23 days
Born: 7 May 1908 in St. Louis, Missouri
Marital Status: Married
Wife: Cassie L Schanz
Occupation: ranching
Died: 11 October 1943 on McNeil Island, Pierce, Washington from Acute serous pleurisy had a thoracentesis operation

103. **Name: Robert Johnson**
Length in time in USP: 2 years 11 months
Born: 4 February 1880 in Houston, Texas
Marital Status: married
Parents: Henry L Johnson and Mary Stewart
Wife: Della Latimer Freeman
Occupation: Farm laborer
Died: 16 April 1944 in McNeil Island, Pierce, Washington from sickle-cell anemia due to Senility and general arteriosclerosis

104. **Name: Leonardo Carrillo-Guajardo**
Length in time in USP: 1 month 21 days
Born: 6 November 1912 in Santo Tomas, Mexico

Marital Status: single
Parents: Sepriano Carrillo and Maria Guajardo
Height: 5 foot 2 inches
Weight: 121 lbs
Hair: black
Complexion: dark
Eyes: dark brown
Occupation: farm labor
Died: 16 October 1945 in McNeil Island, Pierce, Washington from Acute miliary tuberculosis

105. **Name**: **Juan Martinez**
Length in time in USP: 3 months 21 days
Born: 24 June 1907 Hermosillo, Sonora, Mexico
Parents: Leoncio Prado and Cruz Martinez
Height: 5 foot 7 inches
Weight: 184
Hair: black
Complexion: dark
Eyes: brown
Occupation: farmer
Died: 17 July 1946 on McNeil Island, Pierce, Washington from subarachnoid hemorrhage left frontal lobe due to brain tumor

106. **Name**: **William James Paddy**
Length in time in USP: 1 year 9 months 16 days
Conviction: Murder jn Douglas, Alaska
Sentence: 30 August 1942 for life
Born: 25 September 1909 in Haines, Alaska
Parents: Sam Paddy and Annie Eshon
Height: 5 foot 8 inches
Weight: 162 lbs
Hair: black
Complexion: dark
Eyes: black
Occupation: miner and fisherman
Died: 10 March 1947 on McNeil Island, Pierce, Washington from Myocarditis due to Acute rheumatic fever, other conditions Syphilis

107. **Name**: **Walter E McCraye**
Born: 28 December 1897 in Barton, Colerain Township, Belmont, Ohio
Military: yes 1915 to 1919
Marital Status: divorced
Parents: Donald E Horn and Minnie Kelly

Occupation: Construction
Died: 12 May 1950 on McNeil Island, Pierce, Washington from coronary occlusion

108. **Name: Charles Chester McDermott**
Length in time in USP: 1 month
Born: 18 March 1890 in Fort Benton, Chouteau, Montana
Military: yes 1917 to 1918
Parents: Charles McDermott and Margert Ogg
Spouse: Anna Sigrid Kristina Hansen
Height: 5 foot 8 ¾ inches
Weight: 172 lbs
Hair: brown
Complexion: light
Eyes: brown
Occupation:Cook, labor, and pump repairman
Died: 4 October 1950 on McNeil Island, Pierce, Washington from Acute Hemorrhagic,
Pancreatitis due to Aeterio-Sclerotic Heart Disease

109. **Name: Samuel L Fisher**
Length in time in USP: 4 ½ months
Born: 27 February 1880 Chicago, Cook, Illinois
Parents: Henry Fisher and Elizabeth
Occupation: Tailor
Died: 7 December 1950 on McNeil Island, Pierce, Washington from Cachexia due to Gastric
Carcinoma other conditions General debility

110. **Name: Jesus Maria Marin-Torres**
Length in time in USP: 21 months
Conviction: Alien smuggling
Born: 5 October 1902 in Sanchez Roman, Mexico
Marital Status: married
Parents: Antonio M Marin and Josefa Torres
Occupation: farm laborer
Died: 5 May 1951 on McNeil Island, Pierce, Washington from Cerebral Hemorrhage due to
Hypertensive Cardiovascular disease

Jesus persuaded his 14 year old nephew to help smuggle four aliens in the country. The boy
was turned over to his parents,

111. **Name: Tom Ray**
Length in time in USP: 7 months
Born: 1 January 1900 in Kennett, Dunklin, Missouri
Parents: Bob Ray and Fannie Elliott

Height: 5 foot 7 inches
Weight: 135
Hair: brown, gray and bald
Complexion: light
Eyes: blue
Occupation: Laborer
Died: 28 July 1951 on McNeil Island, Pierce, Washington from Ruptured Esophageal Varices due to Cirrhosis of liver

112. **Name**: **Max Joseph Hansen**
Conviction: Burglary
Plead: Guilty
Length in time in USP: 5 ½ months
Born: 3 March 1897 in Washington D C
Military: yes 1916 to 1919
Marital Status: divorced
Parents: Max Hansen and Cassie Condon
Wife: Helen Niewiadomski
Occupation: Painter, plumber, and steamfitter
Died: 5 October 1951 on McNeil Island, Pierce, Washington from Carcinoma of Esophagus other conditions Malnutrition, findings of an operation Carcinoma of Esophagus with Metastasis Witzel Gastrostomy

Max burglarized the Old Country Club building. He stole paint and clothing.

113. **Name**: **Arnold Joseph Schweinfus**
Length in time in USP: 1 year 4 ½ months
Born: 12 March 1897 in Covington, Kenton, Kentucky
Marital Status: Divorced
Parents: Henry J Schweinfus and Catherine Hartke
Wife: Frances Schrichte
Height: 6 foot
Weight: 195 lbs
Hair: black
Complexion: dark
Eyes: blue
Occupation: Machinist
Died: 23 October 1951 on McNeil Island, Pierce, Washington from Broncho-pneumonia other conditions multiple Cerebrovascular accidents

114. **Name**: **James Bernard Anderson**
Length in time in USP: 2 years 3 months
Born: 22 November 1905 in Marquette, Marquette, Michigan

Military: Yes Army 2 February 1922 to 17 February 1925
Marital Status: Divorced
Parents: Louis Ignatius Anderson and Mary J Schmeitzer
Wife: Irene Florence Gorman
Height: 5 foot 11 inches
Weight: 160 lbs
Hair: brown
Complexion: ruddy
Eyes: blue
Occupation: constructor laborer
Died: 7 February 1952 on McNeil Island, Pierce, Washington from Carcinoma of Lung other conditions Cachexia Antecedent causes Uremia

115. **Name: Bruce Goosby Turner**
Length in time in USP: 12 months
Born: 9 April 1917 in Dallas, Collin, Texas
Marital Status: married
Parents: Jess Turner and Mamie Smith
Height: 5 foot 8 inches
Weight: 145
Hair: black
Complexion: dark brown
Eyes: brown
Occupation: laborer
Died: 8 April 1952 on McNeil Island, Pierce, Washington from Hypertension, Malignant

116. **Name: Walter Harvey Horner Wood**
Conviction: interstate transportation of forged securities
Length in time in USP: 9 months
Born: 9 August 1913 in Philadelphia, Pennsylvania
Marital Status: single
Parents: Walter H Wood and Elizabeth Horner
Height: 6 foot ¾ inches
Weight: 150 lbs
Hair: black
Complexion: ruddy
Eyes: blue
Occupation: writer and various others
Died: 6 October 1952 on McNeil Island, Pierce, Washington from Homologous Serum Hepatitis

Walter was part of an experiment seeking a cure for a liver disease. He was one of 200 inmates inoculated with hepatitis. The men offered to help the Army to find a way to combat the ailment, only 15 per cent came down with the disease.

117. **Name: Ronald Leroy Rideout**
Conviction: Robbery
Plead: Guilty
Length in time in USP: 8 months
Born: 17 January 1909 in Van Buren, Aroostook, Maine
Marital Status: single
Parents: Charles M Rideout and Mabel
Height: 5 foot 9 inches
Weight: 141 lbs
Hair: brown
Complexion: ruddy
Eyes: blue
Occupation: varied
Died: 3 December 1952 on McNeil Island, Pierce, Washington from Carcinoma of descending Colon, Metastatic to Liver finds of an operation far advanced Carcinoma of descending colon with extensive hepatic-metastases

Ronald robbed a bank in Iowa a year before getting $870.50. Ronald left in a stolen car, then chartered a plane at a local airport, which he landed in a cornfield in South Dakota, next he hitched a ride into town, and lastly rode a train back to the place he started at in Iowa. At that time his trail went cold. He was arrested a year later in California. Ronald pleaded guilty in California to avoid being sent back to Iowa for trial. When in the bank he tied up the cashier and waited on two patrons, who came in the bank while he robbed it.

118. **Name: Joseph Grobinsky**
Length in time in USP: 2 months 9 days
Born: 12 August 1905 in Poland
Marital Status: single
Parents: Mickael Grobinsky and Francesca
Occupation: cook and caretaker
Died: 26 February 1953 on McNeil Island, Pierce, Washington from Infarction of Myocardium due to Arteriosclerotic heart disease

119. **Name**: **Jack Hinden**
Length in time in USP: 3 ½ months
Conviction: Stealing from a postal mailbox
Born: 13 September 1915 Philadelphia, Pennsylvania
Marital Status: single
Parents: Herman Hinden and Esther
Occupation: baker
Died: 26 June 1953 on McNeil Island, Pierce, Washington from Embryonal Carcinoma (Metastatic) due to Ca of testule

Jack stole a letter out of a mailbox.

120. **Name**: **Antonio Gamboa-Lopez**
Length in time in USP: 1 year
Born: 6 January 1899 in Culiacán, Sinaloa, Mexico
Marital Status: single
Parents: Placebo Gamboa and Ortencia Lopez
Height: 5 feet 6 inches
Weight: 135 lbs
Hair: black
Complexion: dark
Eyes: brown
Occupation: Farm labor
Died: 30 January 1955 on McNeil Island, Pierce, Washington from Acute, Fatal, Coronary Occlusion

121. **Name**: **Joseph Darneal**
Conviction: Robbery
Length in time in USP: 14 months
Born: 11 June 1921 in Cloves, Fresno, California
Military: Yes Navy 4 Nov 1943 to 12 July 1944
Marital Status: Divorced
Parents: James W Darneal and Dorothy Kubala
Wife:Phyllis R Anderson
Height: 6 foot
Weight: 185 lbs
Hair: brown
Complexion: ruddy
Eyes: gray
Occupation: construction roofer and bartender
Died: 31 March 1955 on McNeil Island, Pierce, Washington from Toxicity due to carcinoma of the G I tract

Joseph was arrested within an hour of robbing a bank. He claimed he had no gun, but the teller said she was robbed at gunpoint.

122. **Name**: **Albert Schuh**
Length in time in USP: 12 years
Born: 23 December 1896 in Alt Arzis, Bessarabia, Romania
Marital Status: married
Parents: Friedrich Schuh and Christine Kannewischer
Wife: Martha Hart

Height: 5 foot 10 inches
Weight: 140 lbs
Hair: brown
Complexion: ruddy
Eyes: blue
Occupation: Laborer and farmer
Died: 6 August 1955 on McNeil Island, Pierce, Washington

Albert was arrested after shooting his wife three times. He saw his wife in town with a niece. They have been having domestic problems. He stopped hoping to ask her to work their issues out. He then went back to his truck and pulled out a revolver and shot her three times. Sbe was taken to the hospital in critical condition. They are the parents of 13 children.

123. **Name: Walter Dalton**
Length in time in USP: 3 years
Born: 16 November 1892 in Mount Aries, Surry, North Carolina
Military: yes WWI
Marital Status: single
Parents: Will Haber Dalton and Mattie Harber
Occupation: Janitor
Died: 19 June 1957 on McNeil Island, Pierce, Washington from Aneurysm abdominal Aorta due to Arteriosclerosis other conditions Hypertensive Cardiovascular disease

124. **Name: Edward John Sheridan**
Length in time in USP: 5 months
Born: 29 October 1907 in Leadville, Lake, Colorado
Age when imprisoned
Marital Status: married
Parents: John J Sheridan and Catherine McCarty
Wife: Claire Maloney
Height: 6 foot 1 inch
Weight: 160 lbs
Hair: brown
Complexion: light
Eyes: blue
Occupation: fruit packer and merchant
Died: 22 August 1958 on McNeil Island, Pierce, Washington Acute Coronary occlusion (fatal)

125. **Name: Joseph William Dunaway**
Length of stay in USP: 3 months
Marital Status: Married
Born: 31 July 1921 San Antonio, Texas
Military: WWII 29 September 1941 to 14 September 1943

Parents: Wesley Dunaway
Height: 5 feet 9 inches
Weight: 145 lbs.
Hair: light brown
Complexion: ruddy
Eyes: gray
Occupation: Arc Welder
Died: 12 January 1961 on McNeil Island, Pierce, Washington from unusual response to usual dose of medication that made it an accidental overdose of Paraldehyde for him, due to possible cumulative effect of therapeutic doses of Paraldehyde. Other conditions history of alcoholism, previous use of Paraldehyde, Psychosis

Already have a stone

1. **Name: Joseph Williams Williams**
   Length of stay in USP: 41 months
   Marital status: Married
   Born: 21 February 1892 Boston, Massachusetts
   Military: Yes WWI 17 April 1919
   Parents: Maxwell Williams and Matilda
   Occupation: Auditor in a Hotel
   Died: 29 November 1962 on McNeil Island, Pierce, Washington from Ventricular Fibrillation due to Myocardial Infarction due to Arterioaclereetic cardiovascular Disease

2. **Name: Burris Hankins**
   Conviction: forgery
   Plead: Guilty
   Length of stay in USP: 26 months
   Marital Status: Single
   Born: 1 July 1898 in Marion, Illinois
   Military: Yes in 1917
   Height: 5 foot 9 ½ inches
   Weight: 152 lbs
   Hair: brown gray
   Complexion: dark
   Eyes: brown gray
   Occupation: Construction laborer and carpenter
   Died: 7 February 1964 on McNeil Island, Pierce, Washington from Cardiac arrest due to Myocardial Infarction (Probable)

3. **Name: Everett Hale Hartson**
   Conviction: waterfront pilferage
   Sentence: 10 years

Born: 10 January 1899 Chester, Meigs, Ohio
Military: Yes
Marital Status: married
Parents: Henry Elisher Hartson and Frances Lindley
Wife: Rhea Esther Spangle
Height: 6 foot 1 ½ inches
Weight: 198 lbs
Hair: brown
Complexion: ruddy
Eyes: blue
Occupation: Stevedore and longshoremen
Died: 14 November 1964 on McNeil Island, Pierce, Washington from Cardiac Arrest due to Acute Coronary Occlusion due to Arteriosclerosis heart disease

Everett Has spent many years in prison for burglary and theft. This time he got arrested for taking 18 cases of radios from a waterfront warehouse. It was estimated he had stolen 1500 radios and other items over 3 years.

4. **Name: Mariano Sette Marzan**
    Born: 8 September 1894 in Philippine Island
    Marital Status: Married
    Parents: Siprino Marzan and Olympia Sota
    Wife: Maiccla
    Died: 12 December 1965 on Mt View General Hospital, Tacoma, Pierce, Washington from Bronchopneumonia due to Retroperitoneal hemorrhage due to Dissecting aneurysm of common iliac other conditions miliary tuberculosis
    Buried: 15 December 1965 on McNeil Island, Pierce, Washington

5. **Name: Joseph Luke Anderson**
    Length of stay in USP: 11 months
    Born: 1 October 1863 in Little Rock, Pulaski, Arkansas
    Military: yes US Navy
    Marital Status: Single
    Parents: Luke O Anderson and Lorraine Perusich
    Occupation: Sales - carpentry
    Died: 2 March 1966 on McNeil Island, Pierce, Washington from Cachexia due to cancer of Testicle Embryonal and due to Metastatic to posterior abdominal wall

6. **Name: Walter Lee Case**
    Length of stay in USP: 6 months
    Marital Status: Single
    Born: 7 September 1917 Rogersville, Missouri
    Parents: Samuel Jefferson Case and Nancy Isabell Cornett

Occupation: Construction laborer
Died: 17 May 1966 on McNeil Island, Pierce, Washington from Probable Cerebral Accident (to be determined by autopsy) due to Hypertensive Cardiovascular Heart disease

7. **Name: Saul Solomn Kohn**
Length of stay in USP: 11 months
Born: 27 March 1921 New York City, New York
Military: yes Army 29 December 1942 to 1944
Marital Status: Married
Parents: Carl Kohn and Rose
Height: 5 foot 4 ½ inches
Weight: 127 lbs
Hair: dark brown
Eyes: green
Occupation: com. artist
Died: 25 January 1967 on McNeil Island, Pierce, Washington from Cardiac Arrhythmia due to Arteriosclerotic Heart disease

8. **Name: Anthony George Archondiki**
Alias: Greco
Length of stay in USP: 16 days
Marital Status: Divorced
Born: 26 November 1916 in Chelsea, Massachusetts
Parents: Theodore Archondiki and Irene
Died: 3 May 1967 on McNeil Island, Pierce, Washington from Probable Myocardial Infarction due to ASCVD, Emphysema and Anoxia

9. **Name: U B Eaton**
Conviction: Manslaughter
Sentenced: 1961 for 12 years
Discharged for good behavior: 1964
Born: 17 April 1910 in Bryant, Texas
Marital Status: divorced
Parents: Joe Eaton and Ida
Wife: Loraine
Height: 6 foot
Weight: 155 lbs
Hair: Black
Complexion: Light brown
Eyes: brown
Occupation: construction laborer and Painter
Died: 17 September 1967 on McNeil Island, Pierce, Washington from Cardiorespiratory Failure due to Generalized Pulmonary Emphysema due to Bronchial Asthma

U B was found guilty of a gunshot slaying. He shot a man in the head after they had a fight at an arcade. The man was shot in a car. His body was slumped over the front seat.

10. **Name: John Augustine Coughlin**
Conviction: Robbery and illegal reentry
Length of stay in USP: 6 months
Born: 31 January 1924 Saskatoon, Saskatchewan, Canada
Military: yes 1942 to 1945 and 1946 to 1948
Marital Status: Single
Parents: Leo Joseph Coughlin and Mattie Pike
Occupation: Communication - Radio Announcer
Died: 17 November 1967 on McNeil Island, Pierce, Washington from Cardiac arrest due to respiratory insufficiency, massive pneumonia after right thoracotomy for gunshot of right cheat (50 hours post operative)

John died of a gunshot wound to the chest after trying to escape from prison.

11. **Name: Clifford Arthur Ralph Duhamel**
Born: 24 June 1923 in Rainy River, Ontario, Canada
Marital Status: Separated
Parents: Jean Baptiste Joseph Alexandre Duhamel and Ella May Victoria Lowes
Wife: Erma Agnes Heintz
Occupation: Restaurant owner
Died: 3 April 1968 on McNeil Island, Pierce, Washington from Extension of myocardial infarction with cardiac arrest due to previous myocardial infarction and congestive heart failure due to coronary occlusive disease

12. **Name: Leroy Edward Jones**
Born: 8 June 1922 in Beaver, Beaver, Oklahoma
Marital Status: Single
Parents: Clarence Jones and Della E Colby
Died: 9 May 1968 on McNeil Island, Pierce, Washington from acute coronary artery occlusive due to athesosclesoriac

13. **Name: James Oscar Fadaoff**
Born: 21 January 1932 Kodiak, Alaska
Marital Status: Single
Parents: Nicholai Fadaoff and Ella (true name Fleckla S Balamutoff); step father Mike Chebitnoy
Occupation: Fisherman
Died: 24 April 1969 on McNeil Island, Pierce, Washington from loss of blood due to self inflicted wound of arms and legs due to probable depression

14. **Name: George Washington Durham**
    Born: 5 February 1910 in Des Moines, Polk, Iowa, United States
    Marital Status: Single
    Parents: George W Durham and Mary Edwards
    Height: 6 foot 4 inches
    Weight: 200 lbs
    Hair: brown
    Complexion: ruddy
    Eyes: blue
    Died: 20 November 1970 on McNeil Island, Pierce, Washington from undifferentiated Metastatic due to Carcinoma

15. **Name: John Joseph Powers**
    Alias: Star Power
    Marital Status: Divorced
    Spouse: Frances
    Born: 5 June 1933 Ohio
    Died: 24 February 1971 on McNeil Island, Pierce, Washington from Renal Failure due to Bile peritonitis due to ruptured bile duct

16. **Name: Eric Rudolph Lindberg**
    Conviction: Robbery
    Sentenced: 1969
    Born: 7 May 1924 in Bronx, New York City, New York
    Marital Status: Married
    Parents: Sven Rudolf Lindberg and Hilma Kristina Appel
    Spouse: Billie Claire Armstrong
    Height: 5 foot 8 inches
    Weight: 160 lbs
    Hair: brown
    Complexion: light
    Eyes: brown
    Occupation: Canadian Air Force and Ex Gang Laborer for the railroad, truck driver
    Died: 14 June 1971 on McNeil Island, Pierce, Washington from Thrombosis of right coronary artery artemosolesosis

Eric robbed a bank of $1050. The teller was able to put a teargas bomb into the bag. It was set to go off in 5 minutes. When it went off in a restaurant restroom up the street where he stopped to count the money.

17. **Name: Albert Woodrow Gaunt**
    Born: 14 January 1917 Oklahoma

Marital Status: divorced
Occupation: Office Machine Repair
Died: 19 February 1972 on McNeil Island, Pierce, Washington from Cardiac arrest due to Acute myocardial infarction

18. **Name: Joseph J Dial**
    Born: 21 January 1911 in Dewey, Washington, Oklahoma
    Marital Status: widowed
    Able to read: Yes
    Height: 6 foot
    Weight: 175 lbs
    Hair: brown
    Complexion: ruddy
    Eyes: brown
    Occupation: machinist helper, marine and able bodied Seaman
    Died: 16 December 1972 on McNeil Island, Pierce, Washington from Presumed Cardiac Arrest due to Advanced Arteriosclerotic Heart disease

www.ingramcontent.com/pod-product-compliance
Lightning Source LLC
Chambersburg PA
CBHW081358160726
48000CB00010B/3403